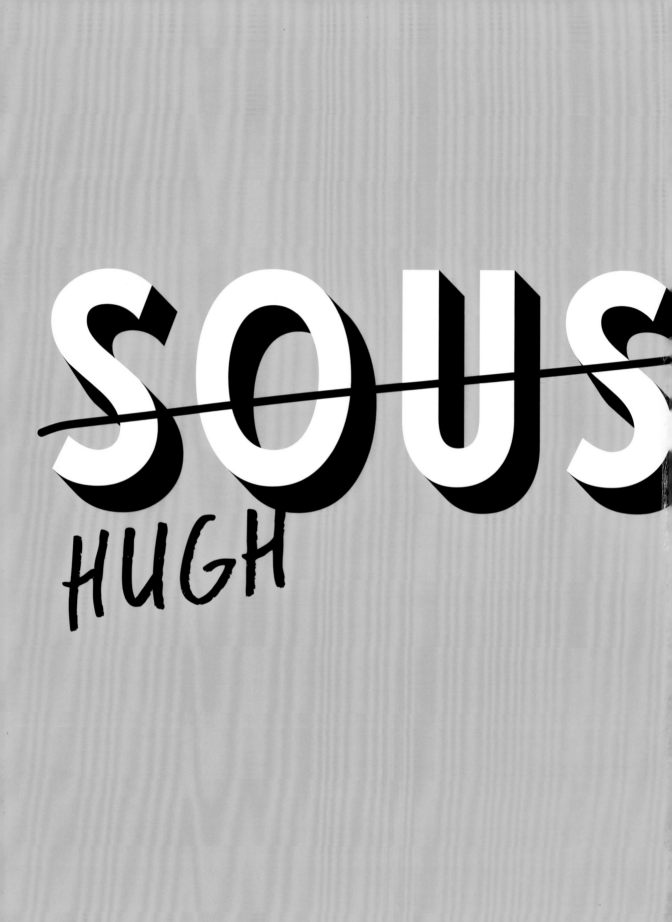

VIDE

Better Home Cooking

Hugh Acheson

Clarkson Potter/Publishers
New York

CONTENTS

There are so many things that you can make—or make better—with sous vide cooking. It opens up new doors for culinary pursuits.

I have been cooking professionally since I was sixteen years old. The past rewarding yet arduous thirty-one years of learning the nuances of food and watching over countless braises, reductions, roasts, and poaches were anchored in teachings that have been culinary bible verse for hundreds of years. Apart from some useful gadgets that have come along, and, I guess, gas and electricity, my cooking techniques are much the same as one would have found in a professional kitchen in France 150 years ago. That timeless foundation has served me well, and changes in food developed at a tectonic pace, at least until fifteen years or so ago.

One of the biggest changes was that "sous vide" became a productive and popular technique for cooking. I remember seeing the cooks in my kitchens starting to use the technology, immersing themselves in the parameters and advantages of cooking food, sealed in bags, in a precisely temperature-controlled water bath. That has never sounded romantic. But the results were impressive, and I was equally impressed with these younger chefs, maybe five to ten years my junior, the first phalanx of a generation who have completely changed the world of food. Watching them learn new techniques has been a wonder; I still look in admiration, and sometimes I feel like the old curmudgeon: "We used to have to cook hundreds of steaks to finally know how to get it medium-rare every single time! Kids these days can just *put it in a bag?* Oh, and I had to walk miles in the snow to get to my fifteen-hour work shift!"

I jest, but some of that is true, save for the walk to work. I usually took the bus. I guess I am just trying to show you how much cooking really has changed in recent years. Technology has completely altered the way we move and act in the kitchen, re-choreographing the dance of line cooking, with the new moves allowing us to precisely achieve temperatures that were a guessing game before. Steam ovens, tilt skillets, induction burners, Cryovac machines and immersion circulators have us culinarily dancing to a different tune.

When sous vide cooking equipment became available to restaurants through a company called PolyScience, the circulators looked like they had been pulled from a steampunk science lab, and, well, they pretty much had been. They initially cost $1,000, and fine dining bought in—hook, line, and sinker—because chefs have a universal yearning to find new ways to produce dishes.

What sous vide did for restaurants was speed up the final execution of food by having much of the food cooked and ready for reheating or a quick sear before service. It guaranteed consistency through accurate cooking temperatures, and reduced food waste through shrinkage during the cooking process. But the sous vide method also had a huge impact on taste. When you learn how to cook a piece of meat or fish (or anything else) in a water bath, understanding the perfect temperature at which the flesh will set up and be cooked but still retain moisture and flavor, you really change how customers eat and how chefs work. For those chefs taking notes on times and temps and homing in on the exact doneness and texture and flavor of the food they were cooking, sous vide was a game changer.

The technology is actually pretty basic when it comes to sous vide, and many thermal circulators have come onto the market. These are essentially thermostat-controlled heating devices with a motor that moves the water around at the precise desired temperature. That's it. But, as with many advances in technology, it takes a while for each new gadget to become commonly available, and I can say this with good experience: My dear father was one of the first people to buy the first IBM home computer, which boasted the processing power of today's toasters for about $20,000. Simple economics shows that more competition drives down prices, and when combined with advances partly in production and partly in technology—well, the price of the circulators is now pretty universally around the $100 to $200 range, and lots of models are available for under $100. You can spend more for commercially robust versions, but the inexpensive ones will get the job done, with aplomb, in a home kitchen.

With so many gadgets, electric pots, fancy ovens, and fridges with Wi-Fi connections, why do you need a sous vide setup in today's world? Well, that is a good question. Although ostensibly a tech gadget, the sous vide circulator is truly a great way to nail old-school cooking. It is a way to efficiently and cleanly make you a better cook, and the often long cook times give you the same freedom that the slow cooker does: the power to walk away from the kitchen and return hours later to a nourishing from-scratch meal.

In fact, sous vide takes that convenience even further: A steak at 129°F is a medium-rare steak, so it can sit in a 129°F water bath for hours and stay a medium-rare steak. You can go run some errands, come back, take a shower, and get that dinner on the table whenever you feel like it. (Okay, okay, technically the steak can't last *forever* at that temperature—it will continue to keep cooking and get mushy-soft if you leave it in there all day—but for most intents and purposes, sous vide will serve to hold your food hot for as long as you need it to.)

And it's not just convenience and precision. There are so many things that you can make—or make better—with sous vide cooking. It opens up new doors for culinary pursuits.

In this book, I share recipes that show some of my favorite characteristics of this method of cooking. I walk you through the basic techniques, and the recipes highlight a whole host of ways sous vide can make your cooking easier, more convenient, and more delicious. It might seem that it's from the future, but really, it's part of the lineage that connects us to the days when humans first discovered cooking. It's a way to get us cooking more, at home, for the people around us.

All you need for sous vide cooking is an immersion circulator (sometimes called a "sous vide machine" or a "sous vide cooker," even though "sous vide" refers to the food being "under vacuum," anyway, I digress . . .), a large vessel to hold the water and mount the circulator on, resealable plastic bags (which are by law food-safe, so don't sweat it!), a clamp or two to attach the bag to the side of the vessel, and some patience as things cook.

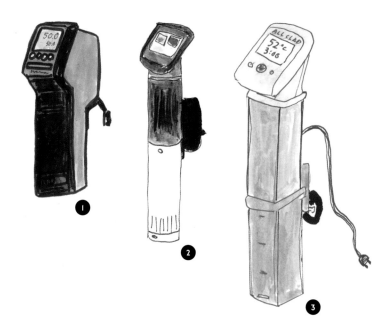

THE CIRCULATOR

Let us begin with the circulator. There are many choices on the market and they all work pretty well. Just look for one that is well built and will last longer than that K-Tel Veg-O-Matic you splurged for in 1978. I don't think you need Wi-Fi connectivity for the unit, which is more and more available, but I guess that could be useful for truly long cooking times, and when you really want to be able to control your cooker through your phone while you're at the movies, but really I think that we are desperately close to societal crumble when we have everything connected to the internet.

I am not recommending any particular brand, but I have used PolyScience ❶, Anova Pro ❷, All-Clad ❸, Nomiku, Joule, and Chefman units with good results. The PolyScience models are the most expensive and are built to hold up in commercial kitchen settings, and the price comparison is much like the relationship between buying a commercial stove versus a home stove. The difference is a unit that can operate under duress for twenty hours every day, compared to a unit that you will use two or three times in a week.

There are some truly inexpensive models coming along, but remember that the difference between inexpensive and cheap is that one implies good value and a smart investment while the other means things will fall apart. The settings on most machines will show temperatures in both Celsius and Fahrenheit, will have a timer, and will have a power button. That really is all you need.

THE WATER BATH

The vessel for the water bath can be a large plastic food-grade container, usually made by Cambro or Rubbermaid, or it can just be a large stockpot with good depth to it. I like the 12-quart size container, which allows for larger things to be cooked comfortably yet doesn't take up a huge amount of counter space. There are specific lids for the plastic food vessels that have a cutout that will accept most circulators, allowing them to retain more heat and prevent the water bath from evaporating away. A lid is not a necessity, but it will accelerate reaching the prescribed temperature setting and insulate it for a consistent water temperature. And, of course, preventing the water from evaporating means it will prevent you from having to check on and replenish the water all the time during a long cook. Instead of a lid, I have also used Ping-Pong balls, spread as a layer on top of the bath (which, believe it or not, created a pretty effective layer of insulation), for the same result. Just using plastic wrap will get you there as well.

As for where to put it, remember that the water bath does produce steam, and if you put the circulator setup on a counter under laminated wood kitchen cabinets and you don't seal it off with a tight lid or plastic wrap, you can slowly ruin the cabinets. Trust me on this one.

THE BAGS

For the cooking pouches, you can use a number of options from freezer zip-top bags, to Cryovac bags, to oven bags. The freezer bags are thicker than regular resealable plastic food bags and less prone to punctures during the cooking process. Cryovac bags are good, too, but without the machine to seal them they are essentially just open-topped pouches. The home versions of Cryovac bags, marketed under the FoodSaver brand, have dimples that affect the texture of the contents, so I do not use them. Commercial Cryovac bags are smooth and are available in different sizes online. For larger items, I often use oven bags, which are heat-resistant bags typically used to cook whole turkeys and other large roasts in the oven. They work fairly well but are pretty thin, so I usually double-bag when using them.

THE CLAMPS

The clamps are just a safety measure to make sure a bag doesn't completely submerge in the bath and possibly take on water. If you are confident in the seal of your bags, you can skip the clamps and just drop the sealed bags into the water bath, but I like to use clamps to keep the tops of the bags out of the water. (Make sure all the *food* in the bags is underwater, though! See more on the method on page 17.) I just use regular large binder clips (the black metal ones) from the office supply store or inexpensive plastic clamps that you would use to close up a half-eaten bag of chips.

THE OTHER KEY STUFF YOU SHOULD HAVE IN YOUR KITCHEN ANYWAY

So the setup for the actual sous vide cooker is pretty simple. Before you use that, though, you will be preparing the food, so let's talk through the basic setup for *mise en place*, the French culinary term for prepping the ingredients and having them in place before you begin to cook.

A good cutting board is your friend. I like heavy wood ones, well washed and sanitized after each use, and liberally swabbed down with mineral oil once a week. (Mineral oil is an edible oil that doesn't go rancid, so stop rubbing your wood cutting board with olive or vegetable oil, because those can spoil and give off an unpleasant scent over time.)

Sharp knives are key to any real cooking. Learn how to sharpen them and learn how to use them. A chef's knife, a boning knife, and a sharp paring knife are your basics. Japanese knives are, to me, the best bet for consistent craftsmanship, but I would not recommend carbon steel knives for home cooks, as they tend to pit and rust easily. Chubo Knives (chuboknives.com) is a great place to peruse Japanese cutlery online.

An inexpensive plastic bowl scraper is a wonderful tool for keeping your cooking area clean. I use them to scoop up diced vegetables and to clean up after mincing herbs. I buy them by the six-pack online. Look for the Ateco 1303. Thank me later.

A spoon larger than a soup spoon and smaller than a typical serving spoon is a chef's friend. It is our spatula, our stirrer, our baster, and the natural extension of the hand. I use the large Gray Kunz spoon available from JB Prince (jbprince.com). You also need a complement of sauce-pans, skillets, and sheet pans, because many times the recipes in this book call for simmer-ing, searing, or broiling. Sheet pans or sheet trays, which are what pros call cookie pans or baking sheets, are essential in half (18 × 13-inch) and quar-ter (9 × 13-inch) sizes. I also like to use small wire racks to hold cooked food that needs to cool and/or rest.

I love mason jars, and some of the recipes call for both quart and half-gallon sizes. Both are commonly available at grocery stores. I use them for storage, for pickling, and for transporting a gift of soup to neighbors and friends.

Kitchen side towels are your new oven mitt, because oven mitts allow for the dexterity of a platypus. Fold a towel into four layers thick and it will protect you from those hot pans. Never use them for that purpose when they are wet, however. Heat transmis-sion through a wet towel is remarkably fast.

Turn the page for a few more things I love having on hand, and that's about it. Let's get sous-viding.

FOLLOWING PAGE

1. Sharpening steel
2. Notebook (I like to document ideas)
3. Small spatula
4. Vegetable peeler
5. Fish bone tweezers
6. Fancy oyster knife
7. Kitchen shears
8. Thermometer
9. Vegetable knife
10. Slicing knife
11. Chef's knife

Vitello Tonnato

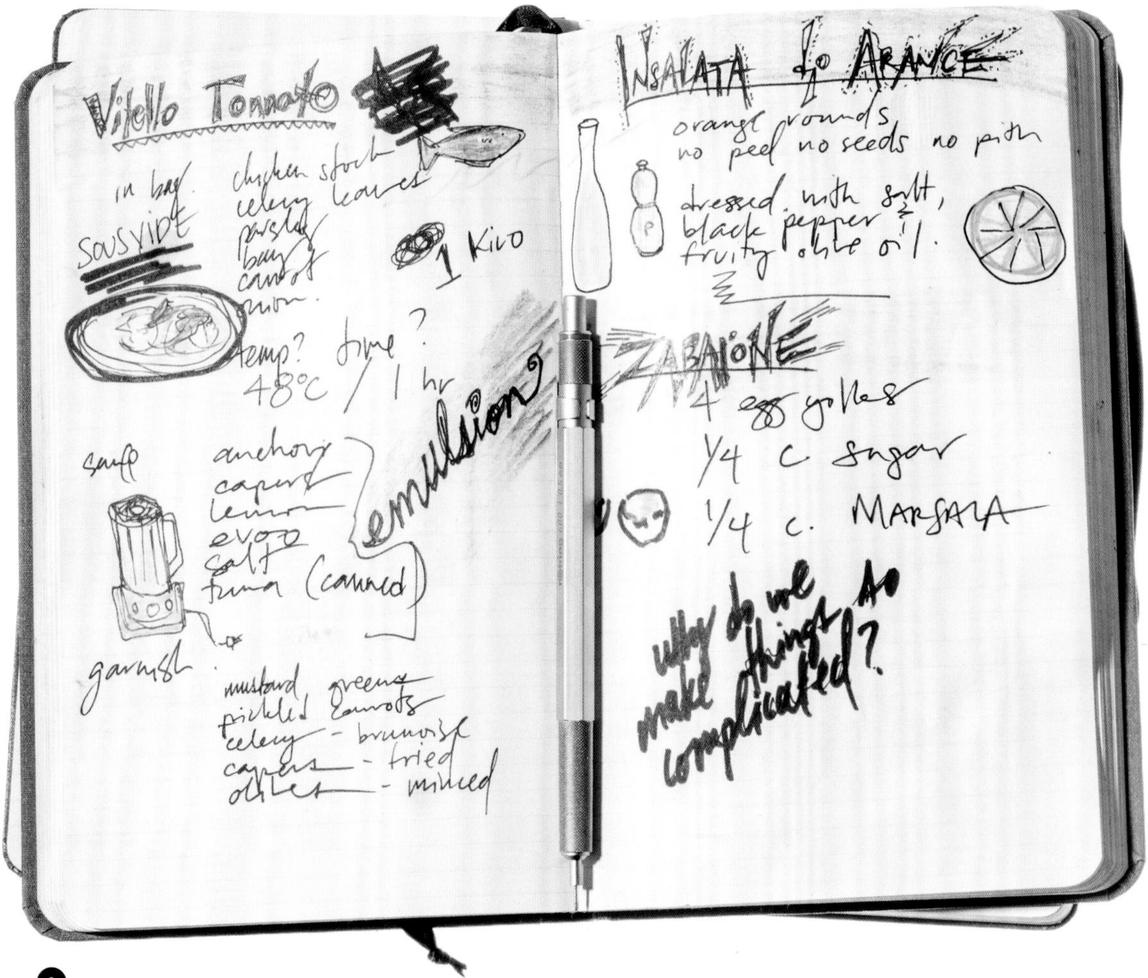

in bag.
SOUSVIDE

chicken stock
celery leaves
parsley
bay
carrot
onion.

1 KILO

Temp? time?
48°C / 1 hr

emulsion

sauce

anchovy
capers
lemon
evoo
salt
tuna (canned)

garnish

mustard greens
pickled carrots
celery — brunoise
capers — fried
olives — minced

INSALATA DI ARANCE

orange rounds,
no peel no seeds no pith

dressed with salt,
black pepper &
fruity olive oil.

ZABAIONE

4 egg yolkes
1/4 c. sugar
1/4 c. MARSALA

why do we make things so complicated?

1

2

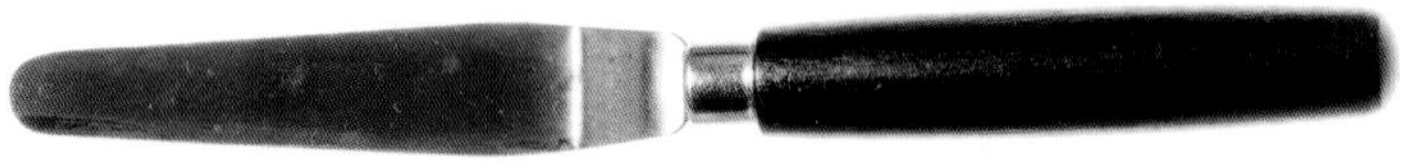

3

4

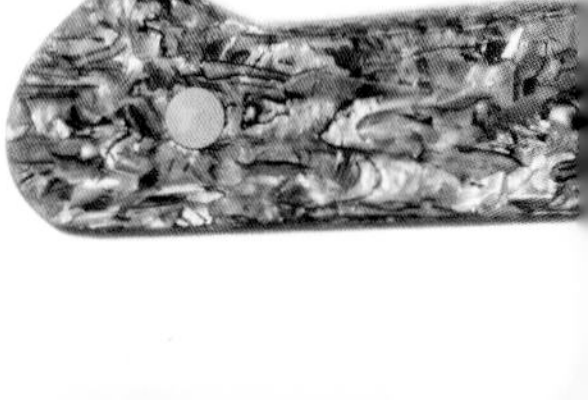

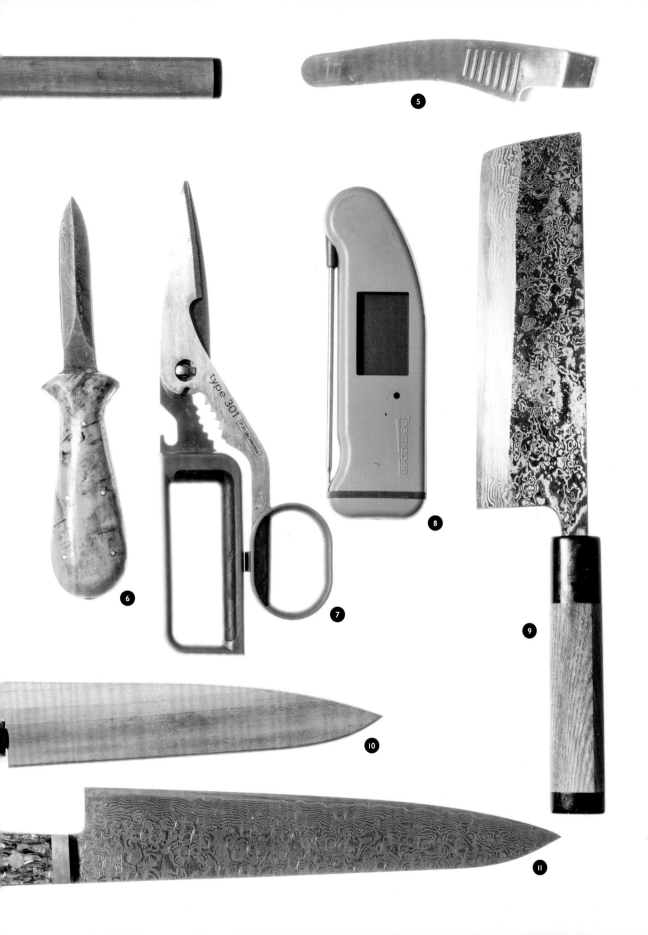

Some books have a long section up front explaining how to go about all the recipes that follow. I will, instead, just give you some basics, as I believe the recipes, um, make sense.

TO BEGIN

Get the sous vide circulator set up and up to temp a little earlier than you might think is necessary, because the temperature can drop a fair bit when you add a bag of cold ingredients, and sometimes the circulators can take a while to get the water up to temperature. You can always cover the water bath with a lid or with plastic wrap to expedite this process. Use water that is at room temperature to start it up, not ice cold. Or, even quicker, use hot water from the tap.

COOK TIMES, HOLDING HOT, AND COOLING

The beauty of sous vide cooking, in addition to the precision it offers, is that you can for the most part hold a piece of food hot, at the exact temperature you want it to be, almost indefinitely after it's done. A medium-rare steak will stay a medium-rare steak for hours, and it won't overcook. So for the most part, once you've cooked something sous vide, you can just let it hang out in the water bath until you're ready to finish and serve it. It makes prepping ahead of time for a dinner or a party much easier.

That said, there are a few caveats. While meat or fish will not "overcook" in the common sense of the word, they do actually continue to change while sitting in the water bath. They will get more tender, like a braise, and eventually get mushy, which is not good. This really only happens after many hours in the bath after the suggested cook time, so realistically it's not going to be an issue for you. But you should know that. (And fruits and vegetables will continue to cook and soften much faster than proteins.)

And if you want to pull the food out of the water bath and chill it for finishing much later, I highly suggest shocking it cold in an ice-water bath, directly in the bag. Cooling food to a safe temperature is critical. For this we use ice baths, but they must be 50 percent ice, and not just a couple of random cubes in lukewarm water. This will chill the food down quickly. Then store it, still in the bag, in the fridge until you are ready to reheat and finish the preparation.

WHY THE BRAND OF SALT MATTERS

When I say "salt," I mean Diamond Crystal kosher salt unless I say otherwise in the particular recipe. I typically have Diamond Crystal kosher salt, sea salt, and a couple of interesting finishing sea salts in my kitchen, but the one that is most important is the kosher—and the specific brand, because I know how it reacts to food, and I know how salty it is. Different brands' salt crystals have different densities, and disparity in a teaspoon of salt from brand to brand is huge, so I just like the benchmark of Diamond Crystal. If you have Morton's kosher salt, though, use one-half to two-thirds of the amount of salt called for in the recipe. Or just salt to taste.

THE DISPLACEMENT METHOD

You will see the "displacement method" mentioned in pretty much every recipe. This is the idea that when you submerge a bag with food inside into a water bath, the air is pushed out of the bag, which in turn allows the food in the bag to stay under the water. It is a branching off from the Archimedes Principle that says—and I am definitely paraphrasing—that any chicken in a bag, when submerged into a body of liquid, will result in an upward buoyant force, the magnitude of which is equal to the weight of the chicken. Get it? That, combined with getting the air out of the bag, will let that chicken sink. Let your chicken sink.

Anyway, the other reason you want to displace the air out of the bag is that the air will act as an insulator, keeping the heat from the water bath away from your food and slowing the whole cooking process down. So: Displace!

If you're using a resealable zip-lock plastic bag, lower the food-filled bag into your water bath and watch the bag close around the food. You can zip the thing shut, leaving an inch or so open so the air can escape, and then zip that last inch once the last bubble of air gets out. Then you can drop the bag into the bath, or clip it, sealed, with a heavy binder clip to the top of the water bath, so that the food is submerged but the top of the bag is still out of the water. This ensures you won't have any open-bag mishaps in the water bath.

Alternatively, or if you're using a big oven bag without a zip-lock, you can lower the bag directly into the circulator water bath for cooking, then use that clip to attach the bag to the side of your water bath, with the food under the water level. You don't need to seal the bag in this case since the airtight part is already under water. Just be sure to clip it really well so the bag doesn't fall in, fill with water, and generally ruin your dinner and make a mess.

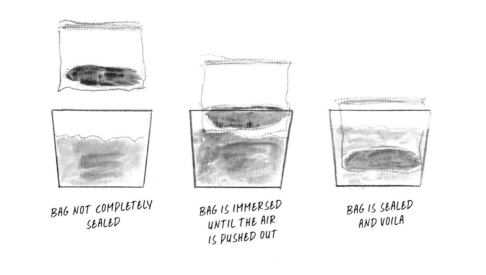

BAG NOT COMPLETELY SEALED

BAG IS IMMERSED UNTIL THE AIR IS PUSHED OUT

BAG IS SEALED AND VOILA

CELSIUS AND FAHRENHEIT

The default cooking temperatures in this book are in Celsius, but I provide Fahrenheit equivalents as well. This is not a Canadian invasion thing. It's simply that Celsius is more common in professional cooking, and thus I have become an adherent. I also use metric a fair bit, mostly when it comes to weights, and that is because metric is brilliant. One liter of water weighs a kilogram! That means a milliliter weighs a gram! Don't get scared—we do use Imperial in this book. But eventually I will completely convert you to metric.

There are more notes and tips throughout the book, but these basics should get you on the right path. Most important, we cook because we seek nourishment, and the process should be a labor of love that makes you smile. So get cooking.

C	F
47	118.4
48	118.4
49	120.2
50	122
51	123.8
52	125.6
53	127.4
54	129.2
55	131
56	132.8
57	134.6
58	136.4
59	138.2
60	140.0
61	141.8
62	143.6
63	145.4
64	147.2
65	149
66	150.8
67	152.6
68	154.4
69	156.2
70	158

C	F
71	159.8
72	161.6
73	163.4
74	165.2
75	167
76	168.8
77	170.6
78	172.4
79	174.2
80	176
81	177.8
82	179.6
83	181.4
84	183.2
85	185
86	186.8
87	188.6
88	190.4
89	192.2
90	194
91	195.8

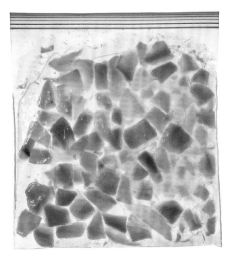

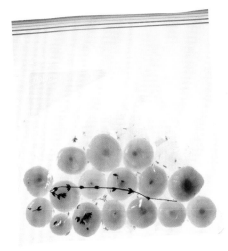

SEAFOOD

Perfectly cooked fish is easy to describe: It is moist and wonderful. Badly cooked fish is dry and sad. Fish is cooked when it becomes opaque; the collagen and connective tissue have melted away, allowing it to flake easily; and the flesh yields easily to the pressure of a fork. Once the sous vide fish is done, you can always add texture by searing or broiling it to get that wonderful golden crust. (In our age of searing obsession, poaching is underrated, but it's the closest traditional technique to sous vide.) The real benefit of sous vide, though, as it always is, is the precise temperature for consistency.

Finding truly great fish can take some searching, but realize that fishmongers still exist in many cities and towns, and you are not solely relegated to the frozen fish selection at the big box store. I do like frozen shrimp in five-pound blocks, though, but buy the domestic ones; other than shrimp, octopus, and squid, I don't buy seafood frozen. Learn the name of the person behind the fish counter, and they will steer you in the right direction for the best in show. Look for clarity of eyes, firmness of flesh, good bright-red bloodlines, translucency in white fish, and a good sheen to the flesh. Ask to smell the fish, and if you're at a place where the fishmonger looks at you strangely for making that request, find another place to shop for your seafood.

Cooking fish sous vide is not a long process. Most fish will cook within an hour, or even just minutes. And the results are stunning. Once you get in the cadence of it, you will never overcook fish again.

COD
with Pimentón Broth and Parsley Gremolata

Prep time: **15 minutes**

Cook time: **30 minutes, plus 10 minutes finishing**

Circulator temperature setting: **51°C / 123.8°F**

SERVES 4

4 cod fillets (5 ounces each), about 1 inch thick

1 teaspoon fine sea salt

2 tablespoons unsalted butter

½ pound Portuguese chouriço (or Spanish chorizo), diced

2 shallots, minced

½ teaspoon pimentón dulce (see Note)

½ cup canned diced tomatoes

3 garlic cloves, finely minced

2 cups fino sherry

2 red bell peppers, roasted, peeled, and seeded (see page 80)

4 cups chicken stock (page 188)

2 tablespoons extra-virgin olive oil, plus more for finishing

Parsley Gremolata (recipe follows)

Smoked paprika: Eastern European paprika is familiar to us all, but I want you to fall in love with the Spanish version: *pimentón de la vera*. Hungarian paprika is sweet and redolent, but it lacks the Spanish version's smoke, a result of drying the peppers very slowly over oak fires. There are three types of pimentón: picante (hot), agridulce (bittersweet), and dulce (sweet). Pimentón is the backbone of many classic Spanish culinary preparations like paella, sofrito, and chorizo. You can buy great versions at good groceries—just make sure you understand the difference between picante and dulce.

Cod is my fish. It has fed my people for five hundred years. I am Canadian and cod fishing is the livelihood for many in the eastern provinces. The story of cod is a painful one, though. Vast overfishing caused depletion, and a difficult twenty years of moratoriums on fishing for cod was economically crushing. But that pause worked, and cod stocks have come back in relative abundance; combined with more sustainable fishing practices, like hand lines as opposed to bottom trawlers, we can eat cod with pride again. Just know where your fish comes from, and choose the line-caught stuff.

The Portuguese have long fished in those Canadian waters, too, and though that has caused some disdain from the locals for centuries, it also has eloquently influenced the foodways of that region. This is a dish of classic flavors from the Iberian larder.

1. Preheat the circulator water bath to 51°C / 123.8°F

2. Dry the cod fillets well with a paper towel and season them with ½ teaspoon of the salt. Place the fillets in a resealable gallon-size plastic bag and seal the bag using the displacement method (see page 17). Submerge the bag in the circulator water bath and cook for 30 minutes; after that, you can hold it there hot until you're ready to finish.

3. Twenty minutes before serving, add the butter to a large skillet set over medium heat. When the butter begins to froth and bubble, add the chouriço and cook until it begins to brown and crisp, about 4 minutes. Remove a few slices and reserve for garnish. Add the shallots, pimentón, and diced tomatoes and cook for 4 minutes, or until the mixture looks like a cooked-down sofrito and is redolent with the aromas of shallot and paprika. Stir, add the garlic,

⟫➤ *Recipe continues*

and cook for 2 minutes more. Deglaze the pan with the sherry and stir again. Add the roasted red peppers and the chicken stock and season with the remaining ½ teaspoon salt. Bring to a simmer and cook until the flavors are well incorporated, about 10 minutes.

4. Transfer the chouriço mixture to a blender and purée until it is just smooth. Strain the purée through a fine-mesh sieve set over a medium saucepan to reserve the broth, and discard any solids. Cover the pan with a lid and keep the broth warm.

5. Remove the bag from the hot water bath and transfer the cod to a plate lined with paper towels, discarding any cooking liquid. Pat the fillets dry with a paper towel.

6. Add the oil to a large skillet set over medium-high heat. When the oil starts to shimmer, add the cod fillets. Cook for 4 minutes on one side, without moving them too much, to get a nice golden-brown color. Transfer the fillets, seared-side up, to a cooling rack or to a plate lined with paper towels to rest for 2 to 3 minutes.

7. To serve, place the fillets in separate wide bowls. Spoon the warm pimentón broth over the fillets and garnish each serving with a spoonful of the parsley gremolata, the reserved chouriço, and a drizzle of olive oil.

PARSLEY GREMOLATA
Makes about ½ cup

½ cup fresh flat-leaf parsley leaves, minced

1 garlic clove, minced

2 tablespoons finely grated lemon zest

1 tablespoon freshly squeezed lemon juice

2 tablespoons extra-virgin olive oil

Fine sea salt

In a small bowl, mix together the parsley, garlic, lemon zest, lemon juice, and olive oil. Season with salt to taste and stir to combine. This will keep, covered, in the fridge for only about a day, so make it fresh.

PICKLED OYSTERS

with Aguachile, Avocado, and Citrus

Prep time: **30 minutes**

Cook time: **20 minutes**

Circulator temperature setting: **48.9°C / 120°F**

SERVES 4 TO 6

2 serrano chiles, stemmed, coarsely chopped (serranos are pretty hot; adjust the amount to your taste)

2 tablespoons chopped fresh cilantro leaves

½ cup freshly squeezed lime juice (from about 4 limes)

Kosher salt and freshly ground black pepper

24 oysters, shucked

2 grapefruits, cut into supremes (see below)

2 oranges, cut into supremes (see below)

1 avocado, thinly sliced

½ red onion, very thinly sliced, for garnish

Avocado oil or extra-virgin olive oil, for finishing

———

Supremes are the pith-free sections of citrus. Extracting them is a bit of a task, but when you have the knife dexterity to do it quickly and safely, you will have risen in Jedi rank. Cut away the top ½ inch of the citrus fruit, and then the bottom ½ inch. From there you can see where the white pith begins. Carve the skin and pith away as though you were whittling the fruit down. Once all the outer pith is removed, take the fruit in the palm of your hand and very carefully cut each segment away from the membranes that hold it in. Save the segments, now called supremes, and squeeze any juice on top of them. Got it? If not, go watch YouTube.

I grew up eating canned smoked oysters. I loved them. They were our treat. Granted, I was a strange child.

These oysters, lightly pickled in the manner of escabèche, are served with a simple chile water with avocado and citrus fruit. It is a beautiful course for those months that end in R, but you can probably eat a variation of it year round.

1. Preheat the circulator water bath to 48.9°C / 120°F.

2. Place the serrano chiles, 1 tablespoon of the cilantro, ¼ cup of water, and the lime juice in a blender. Blend until smooth. Season with salt and pepper to taste. This is your aguachile.

3. Place the oysters and the aguachile in a resealable gallon-size plastic bag. Sink the bag into the circulator water bath, using the displacement method to ensure they are under the water line (see page 17). Cook the oysters for 20 minutes.

4. Remove the bag from the hot water bath and transfer the oysters and the aguachile to a medium bowl. They can be chilled or served warm. If you chill them in the aguachile, they will stay fresh for about 3 days, but the acid will continue to firm them up, like a ceviche.

5. Layer the grapefruit and orange supremes with the avocado slices on 4 plates. Spoon 6 oysters and some of the aguachile over the avocado and citrus. Garnish with the red onion, remaining 1 tablespoon cilantro, and the avocado oil. Season with salt and pepper to taste.

SALMON

with Dill, Shallot, Lemon, and Vermouth

Prep time: **8 hours brine time plus 10 minutes prep**

Cook time: **30 minutes, plus 5 minutes finishing**

Circulator temperature setting: **48°C / 118°F**

SERVES 4

4 salmon fillets (5 to 6 ounces each), 1 inch thick at the thickest point, with or without skin

4 cups Basic Brine (recipe follows)

1 shallot, minced

1 cup dry white vermouth

1 teaspoon freshly squeezed lemon juice

3 tablespoons unsalted butter

2 tablespoons minced fresh dill stems

Kosher salt

1 teaspoon extra-virgin olive oil

¼ cup fresh dill fronds

If you can get great wild salmon, buy it. Wild is the best choice for taste, sustainability, and provenance. Though there are well-farmed options, finding them requires some due diligence and investigation. Norway, Ireland, and British Columbia have some great marine pen systems that seem to operate well—meaning that they don't poison the surrounding water with feed and feces, and they don't let the farmed fish escape into the wild. (They don't have the ability to survive in the wild, which is bad; but even worse, when they mate with wild fish, they create offspring that can't survive.) Sadly, even the good systems are not yet perfect, and both issues of are constant concern.

This recipe involves a number of steps but results in a beautiful plate of food. Brining the salmon will season the fish evenly through, firm the flesh a bit, and also reduce the extrusion of albumin when you finish it in the pan. (Albumin is the white protein that is pushed out of fish during cooking, but in perfectly cooked fish, you shouldn't see it.) Here we show you how.

1. You must brine before you dine. Eight hours before you plan to eat, submerge the salmon fillets in the brine.

2. Preheat the circulator water bath to 48°C / 118°F.

3. Remove the salmon fillets from the brine and pat them dry with paper towels. Place them in a resealable gallon-size plastic bag and seal it using the displacement method (see page 17). Submerge the bag in the circulator water bath. Cook for 30 minutes; after that, you can hold it there hot until you are ready to finish the dish.

4. When the salmon is about 10 minutes from being done, start your sauce: In a small saucepan combine the shallot, vermouth, and lemon juice. Place the pan over medium-high heat, bring the mixture to a boil, and reduce for about 5 minutes, or until the vermouth is reduced by about two-thirds. Remove the pan from the heat, slowly whisk in the butter, and finish with the dill stems. Season with salt to taste.

5. Preheat your broiler on high.

6. Remove the bag from the hot water bath and carefully transfer the salmon fillets to clean paper towels and blot them dry. Discard the paper towels and place the salmon on a sheet pan, skin-side up if it has skin. Drizzle with the olive oil and broil for 2 to 3 minutes, until lightly browned. Transfer the salmon to plates and spoon the sauce over each portion. Garnish with the dill fronds.

BASIC BRINE

Makes 1 liter (just over a quart)

This brine is a 5 percent saline solution, meaning the salt content weighs 5 percent of the weight of the water. Thus it contains 50 grams of salt to 1,000 grams of water, which is 1 kilogram, which is 1 liter of water. Brilliant. But since people in America are for some reason still wary of the metric system, despite the fact that it makes so much sense, in this recipe we are mixing Imperial and metric systems like a patois of two languages.

Brine will keep for a couple of weeks in the fridge, so you can make a double batch if you find yourself eating a lot of salmon, which your doctor would probably encourage. (Toss the brine after you've used it, though.)

50 grams salt (4 tablespoons Diamond Crystal kosher salt)

1 liter water (or 1 quart plus ¼ cup)

1 teaspoon coriander seeds

Pinch of whole black peppercorns

1 sprig fresh thyme

Combine the salt, water, coriander seeds, peppercorns, and thyme sprig in a medium saucepan, and bring to a boil to fully dissolve the salt. Remove the pan from the heat and let the brine cool to room temperature before using.

SWORDFISH

with Coconut Green Curry Sauce

Prep time: **20 minutes**

Cook time: **30 minutes, plus 5 minutes finishing**

Circulator temperature setting: **55°C / 131°F**

SERVES 4

2 **tablespoons** grated fresh ginger

2 **tablespoons** thinly sliced lemongrass (see Note)

3 **tablespoons** sliced scallions, white and light green parts only

1 serrano chile, stemmed

2 shallots

½ **teaspoon** coriander seeds, toasted

½ **teaspoon** cumin seeds, toasted

2 **cups** freshly chopped cilantro leaves and stems, 2 **tablespoons** of the whole leaves reserved

¼ **cup** freshly squeezed lime juice (from about 3 limes)

2 **tablespoons** fish sauce

1 **(13.5- to 14-ounce) can** unsweetened coconut milk

4 swordfish steaks (5 ounces each)

Kosher salt and freshly ground black pepper

2 **tablespoons** extra-virgin olive oil

¼ **cup** salted peanuts, toasted and chopped

Note: The tender, flavorful parts of the lemongrass stalk are what you want. Peel off the first couple layers of dry leaves. Slice from the bottom of the stalk, using the pale-colored parts, usually about the bottom 3 inches. The rest of the stalk you can use to infuse into stocks or to make tea.

I love meaty, steaklike seafood, and swordfish is at the apex of that style of fish. This sauce is Thai in style, but thoroughly achievable. I say that because Thai food can contain seventy ingredients in a dish. This has about a dozen ingredients and still packs a ton of flavor. Swordfish likes to be cooked, but not overcooked, since it doesn't have much fat to it. So 55°C / 131°F it is, more medium than medium-rare.

1. Preheat the circulator water bath to 55°C / 131°F.

2. Place the ginger, lemongrass, scallions, serrano, shallots, coriander, cumin, 2 cups cilantro, lime juice, and fish sauce in a blender and purée until a nice paste is achieved. (Add a bit of water if it's too thick.)

3. Heat the curry paste in a medium saucepan over medium heat. Whisk in the coconut milk and bring the mixture up to a simmer. Reduce the heat to low and cover; let sit to allow the flavors to meld.

4. Season the swordfish with salt and pepper. Place in a single layer in a resealable gallon-size plastic bag. Seal the bag using the displacement method (see page 17). Immerse it in the circulator water bath and cook for 30 minutes; after that, hold it there until you're ready to finish. Remove the bag from the hot water bath, transfer the swordfish to a plate lined with paper towels, and blot it very dry.

5. In a cast-iron skillet, heat the oil over medium-high heat. Once the oil starts to shimmer, sear the swordfish for 2 minutes on each side to get a nice brown. Place the steaks on a rack or on a plate lined with (fresh) paper towels.

6. To serve, spoon the curry sauce into a large wide bowl or a high-lipped plate. Place the seared swordfish steaks in the curry sauce, and garnish with the chopped peanuts and the reserved 2 tablespoons cilantro leaves.

SEAFOOD **33**

TUNA VENTRESCA
with Italian Salad

Prep time: **30 minutes**

Cook time: **30 minutes**

Circulator temperature setting: **58°C / 136.4°F**

SERVES 4

For the tuna

¾ pound ahi (aka yellowfin) tuna belly

1 cup extra-virgin olive oil

1 cup grapeseed oil

½ teaspoon fine sea salt

Pinch of crushed red pepper flakes

1 teaspoon minced fresh thyme leaves

For the salad

½ cup extra-virgin olive oil

3 tablespoons red wine vinegar

1 tablespoon mayonnaise

1 teaspoon dried oregano

1 garlic clove, minced

1 teaspoon kosher salt

Freshly ground black pepper

2 cups chopped iceberg lettuce

2 medium-size heirloom tomatoes

¼ cup fresh flat-leaf parsley leaves

½ cup sliced pepperoncini

Ventresca is preserved tuna belly, popular in Spain, Portugal, and Italy. The tuna is slowly cooked in olive oil and then stored within the oil. You usually see it canned, because the Iberian peninsula is the OG of quality tinned seafood. This version uses poached fresh tuna, served warm with a very zesty American-Italian-style salad. Think *Goodfellas* red-checked-tablecloth-style salad. I love iceberg lettuce. And a warning: This salad is totally addictive.

Finding tuna that makes you happy means finding a happy fishmonger. I am an advocate of building a trust relationship with purveyors who really love selling great product. They are out there, and the relationship is built on you being a consistent customer, getting to know them, and thanking them often for being a filter against ho-hum seafood. If you can't find belly, tuna loin will work fine. It is not as supple and rich, but it is still very tasty.

1. Preheat the circulator water bath to 58°C / 136.4°F.

2. Cut the tuna into 4 relatively evenly sized rectangles. Place the tuna in a resealable gallon-size bag. In a small bowl, whisk together the olive oil, grapeseed oil, sea salt, red pepper flakes, and thyme, and pour the mixture into the bag. Seal the bag using the displacement method (see page 17). Immerse the bag in the circulator water bath and cook for 30 minutes.

3. While the tuna cooks, let us prep the vinaigrette and the salad: Place a clean small mason jar on the counter. Into the jar goes the olive oil, red wine vinegar, mayonnaise, oregano, garlic, ½ teaspoon of the kosher salt, and a heady amount of pepper. Cap the jar securely and shake it vigorously for 1 minute. This is a workout, but you need to emulsify the mayo into everything else. It won't stay emulsified forever, but no biggie. Shake it up when you need it.

Place the lettuce in a large salad bowl. Cut the tomatoes into 1-inch rough cubes, and season with the remaining ½ teaspoon salt. Add the tomatoes, parsley leaves, and sliced peppers to the lettuce.

When the tuna is done, remove the bag from the hot water bath, transfer the tuna to a paper towel–lined plate, and let it cool for 5 minutes. Discard the poaching oil. Then break the tuna up a touch and add it to the salad bowl. Add the vinaigrette to your liking, toss gently, and serve.

TUNA
with Ratatouille Salsa

Prep time: **20 minutes**

Cook time: **30 minutes for eggplant, 12 minutes for tuna, plus 10 minutes finishing**

Circulator temperature setting: **85°C / 185°F for eggplant, then 50°C / 122°F for tuna**

SERVES 4

1 cup small-diced globe eggplant

3 tablespoons extra-virgin olive oil

2 bay leaves

1½ teaspoons kosher salt

1 sprig fresh thyme

1 cup diced fresh heirloom tomato

1 cup finely diced yellow squash

1 cup finely diced red bell pepper

2 garlic cloves, minced

¼ cup fresh small basil leaves

4 ahi (yellowfin) tuna steaks
  (4 ounces each)

Freshly ground black pepper

1 tablespoon unsalted butter

1 tablespoon canola oil

In my dream, this is a midsummer early evening meal. I am in rural Provence, outside next to vineyards, sipping rosé at a long table covered with a colorful tablecloth and unmatched china. I am speaking French better than I actually do. I am not wearing a beret, but wish I were, as all of my favorite people are at the table, all wearing berets. I will come better prepared to my dream next time.

Ratatouille is a quintessential ode to Provence: a quartet of tomatoes, eggplant, peppers, and squash, brought into line by basil and a substantial amount of olive oil. This salsa is inspired by that dish, with the vegetables finely cut and the texture of the eggplant controlled by cooking it first and then by searing it.

1. Preheat the circulator water bath to 85°C / 185°F.

2. Place the eggplant, 1 tablespoon of the olive oil, the bay leaves, and ½ teaspoon of the salt in a resealable gallon-size plastic bag and seal it using the displacement method (see page 17). Immerse it in the circulator water bath and cook for 30 minutes.

3. Meanwhile, combine the thyme sprig, tomato, squash, red bell pepper, and garlic in another resealable gallon-size plastic bag, and add 1 tablespoon of the oil and ½ teaspoon of the salt. Mix it up with a spoon and seal that bag as above. Immerse it in the water bath next to the eggplant, and cook for 20 minutes.

4. Remove both bags and reduce the circulator setting to 50°C / 122°F. Separately, strain the eggplant and the tomato mixture, discarding whatever cooking liquids have accumulated. Place the eggplant in one bowl and the tomato mixture in another.

≫→ *Recipe continues*

5. Heat the remaining 1 tablespoon oil in a large skillet set over medium-high heat. When the oil is shimmering, add the eggplant and sear it for about 2 minutes, until it has developed a golden-brown color. Remove the skillet from the heat and add the eggplant to the tomato mixture. Add the basil leaves and toss well. Set the salsa aside and wipe out the skillet.

6. When the circulator temperature has lowered to 50°C / 122°F, we can cook the tuna: Season the tuna steaks with the remaining ½ teaspoon salt and with pepper to your liking, and place them in a resealable gallon-size plastic bag. Add the butter to the bag, seal as above, and immerse it in the circulator bath. Cook for 12 minutes and then remove the bag from the hot water bath. Transfer the tuna to a plate and pat the steaks dry with a paper towel.

7. Place the large skillet you cooked the eggplant in over medium-high heat. Add the canola oil and raise the heat to high. When the oil comes to a light smoke, swirl it around to cover the pan and add the tuna steaks to the hot pan. Sear for 1 minute per side, until golden brown, and then transfer the tuna to a cutting board.

8. Cut each portion of tuna in half and place them on a large platter. Finish with a copious amount of the ratatouille salsa. Serve.

SARDINES ESCABÈCHE

Prep time: **30 minutes**

Cook time: **30 minutes**

Circulator temperature setting: **51°C / 123.8°F**

SERVES 4

6 whole fresh sardines

Kosher salt

¾ cup extra-virgin olive oil

4 bay leaves

½ carrot, thinly sliced

½ shallot, thinly sliced

1 teaspoon minced fresh thyme leaves

Pinch of crushed red pepper flakes

½ cup finely minced fresh parsley leaves and stems

Grated zest and juice of 1 lemon

1 tablespoon cider vinegar

¼ cup halved cherry tomatoes

Fine sea salt

Escabèche refers to cooked fish that is marinated—after it's cooked—in a vinegar sauce. Sardines are a classic with this preparation, but it will work with pretty much any small fish like red mullet, fresh anchovies, even small trout.

This recipe makes a great shared plate in a summer supper scenario. I wouldn't say it is an appetizer, but rather a part of a spread. I think the rest of the spread to be a salad, some simple steamed potatoes, prosciutto, summer melon, and a crisp bottle of Chenin Blanc. Dinner is served.

1. Preheat the circulator water bath to 51°C / 123.8°F.

2. Using a small paring knife, cut off the head of each sardine. Slice the belly open and gut the fish. Pull out the center bone; the rib cage will come out as well. Season the fish with kosher salt inside and out.

3. Place the sardines in a resealable gallon-size plastic bag and add 1 tablespoon of the oil along with the bay leaves, carrot, shallot, and thyme. Seal the bag using the displacement method (see page 17). Submerge the bag in the circulator water bath and cook for 30 minutes.

4. While the sardines are hanging out in their bath, let's make the escabèche: Pour the remaining oil into a small saucepan and add the red pepper flakes, parsley, lemon zest, lemon juice, and cider vinegar. Cook over medium heat until the flavors have all mingled together, about 5 minutes. Add the tomatoes, remove the saucepan from the heat, and cool to room temperature.

5. Carefully remove the sardines from the bag and place them on a cutting board to cool. Reserve the carrots and shallots and discard the bay leaves. Arrange the sardines, carrots, and shallots on a plate and then sauce up with the vinaigrette and the tomatoes. Season with a pinch of fine sea salt, or more as desired.

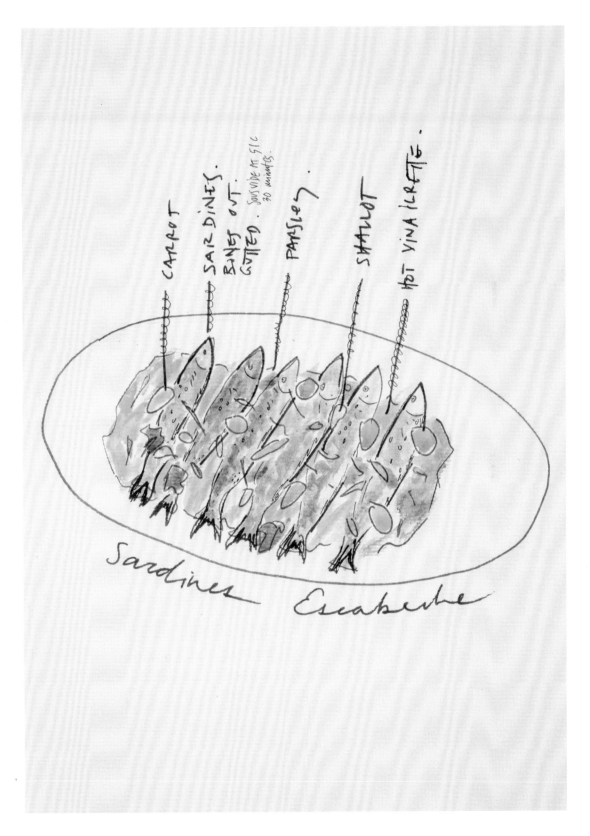

CARROT

SARDINES.
BONES OUT.
GUTTED. Sous vide m SLC
30 minutes.

PARSLEY.

SHALLOT

HOT VINAIGRETTE.

Sardines Escabeche

HALIBUT

with Carrot-Ginger Sauce and Hazelnut-Carrot Salad

Prep time: **15 minutes**

Cook time: **30 minutes, plus 5 minutes finishing**

Circulator temperature setting: **48°C / 118.4°F**

SERVES 4

- **4** center-cut halibut fillets (6 ounces each), skin removed
- **1 teaspoon** kosher salt, plus more to taste
- **4 sprigs** fresh thyme
- **½ cup** sliced young carrots (in ½-inch-thick rounds), plus 4 whole small carrots
- **1 tablespoon** minced fresh ginger
- **1 cup** dashi (page 193)
- **3 tablespoons** cold unsalted butter
- **¼ cup** chopped well-washed carrot tops
- **2 tablespoons** chopped fresh flat-leaf parsley leaves
- **2 tablespoons** chopped fresh mint leaves
- **1 tablespoon** fresh tarragon leaves
- **2 tablespoons** lightly crushed toasted hazelnuts
- **2 tablespoons** extra-virgin olive oil
- **1 tablespoon** freshly squeezed lemon juice
- Fine sea salt

This is a simple marriage of four unique flavors that work really well together: the firm, beautiful flesh of halibut, the piquant assertiveness of ginger, the mellow sweetness of carrots, and the smoky crunch of hazelnuts. Get them all at peak quality, and you have a winner of a dish that is so easy to prepare.

This is the plan: We will get the fish poaching, make the sauce while that is happening, and assemble the makings of the finishing salad. When the fish is done, we will pop it into the broiler to give it a little color and then plate everything up. Serve the dish with a bottle of white Burgundy and enjoy the evening.

Pet peeve: Young carrots are not the "baby" carrots you find in lunch bags across the land. Those "baby" carrots are actually large commodity carrots, honed down to little-kid size, washed with a preservative, and packed months ago. Buy real carrots with the greens attached.

1. Preheat the circulator water bath to 48°C / 118.4°F.

2. Place the halibut on a sheet pan and season the pieces all over with the teaspoon of kosher salt. Place the halibut in a resealable gallon-size plastic bag and add the thyme sprigs. Seal the bag using the displacement method (see page 17). Immerse the bag in the circulator water bath and cook for 30 minutes; after that, you can hold it there hot until you're ready to finish.

3. About 15 minutes before serving, combine the ½ cup young carrots, ginger, and dashi in a small saucepan. Cook over medium heat until the carrots are just tender, about 10 minutes. Season the mixture with a pinch of kosher salt and transfer it to a blender. While the mixture is still hot, purée until it is very smooth. While the blender is still running, add 2 tablespoons of the butter through that little hole in the lid. Return the sauce to the saucepan and keep it warm until ready to serve.

4. Cut the remaining 4 small carrots into thick rounds, and combine them in a mixing bowl with the chopped carrot tops, parsley, mint, tarragon, and hazelnuts. Dress with the olive oil and lemon juice and season to taste with fine sea salt.

5. When you're ready to serve, fire up the broiler on high. Grease a baking pan with the last tablespoon of butter. Remove the halibut from the bag, pat it dry with paper towels, and lay the pieces on the baking pan. Broil until lightly browned, 2 to 3 minutes. Serve immediately with the carrot-ginger purée alongside and top the fish with the carrot salad.

SOLE

with Capers, Lemon, and Garlicky Bread Crumbs

Prep time: **15 minutes**

Cook time: **10 minutes, plus 10 minutes finishing**

Circulator temperature setting: **51°C / 123.8°F**

SERVES 4

4 thick fillets of sole (6 ounces each)

Kosher salt

3 tablespoons unsalted butter

1 tablespoon extra-virgin olive oil

1 tablespoon all-purpose flour

2 tablespoons fresh bread crumbs (see below)

1 garlic clove, minced

1 shallot, minced

½ cup dry white vermouth

Grated zest and juice of 1 lemon

1 teaspoon chopped fresh parsley leaves

2 tablespoons capers

¼ cup chicken stock (page 188)

Making bread crumbs: Making bread crumbs is easy, and you can freeze them in batches to keep them fresh. The process is to really dry out the bread, rather than toasting it, and contrary to belief, fresh bread, not stale, makes better crumbs. Cut the bread up into small cubes and place them in one layer on a baking pan. Bake in a 110°C/225°F oven for 30 minutes or so. Then pulse the cubes into crumbs in a food processor. Pack the crumbs up in single-cup measures in small plastic bags and freeze until needed.

This is based on the classic recipe for *sole à la meunière*—sole with a buttery lemon and parsley sauce. The sole should be on the thicker side, about ¾ to 1 inch thick. On a flatfish, the side that faces the light, which is the gray side, is usually thicker. I am not a marine biologist, so don't ask me why. I am a chef and can tell you that the initial cook in the water bath will result in you nailing the temperature.

1. Preheat the circulator water bath to 51°C / 123.8°F.

2. Season the fish with salt and place in a resealable gallon-size plastic bag. Add 1 tablespoon of the butter and seal the bag using the displacement method (see page 17). Submerge the bag in the circulator water bath and cook for 10 minutes; after that you can hold it there hot until you are ready to finish. Remove the bag from the hot water bath and transfer the fish to a plate. Pat it dry with a paper towel.

3. Heat the oil in a 12-inch skillet over medium-high. Dust the sole with the flour. When the oil begins to shimmer, add the sole and cook for 1 minute, just on one side. Add 1 tablespoon butter to the pan and cook for 2 minutes on the same side, until golden brown. Transfer the fish to a platter, golden side up, and keep the butter in the skillet.

4. Reduce the heat to medium. Add the bread crumbs and toast them, stirring frequently, 2 minutes. Add the garlic and cook for 1 minute. Spoon the bread crumb mixture evenly over the sole fillets. Return the skillet to medium heat. Add 1 tablespoon butter, and when it foams, add the shallot and cook until it is translucent, about 1 minute. Deglaze the pan with the vermouth. Cook it down for 1 minute and add the lemon zest and juice, parsley, capers, a pinch of salt, and the chicken stock. Stir, and cook for 2 minutes or until combined. Spoon the sauce over the sole and serve.

FLOUNDER

with Corn, Tomato, and Basil

Prep time: **10 minutes**

Cook time: **20 minutes, plus 10 minutes finishing**

Circulator temperature setting: **51°C / 123.8°F**

SERVES 4

4 flounder fillets (5 ounces each), skin off (see Note)

1 **teaspoon** kosher salt

1 **tablespoon** unsalted butter

2 **tablespoons** extra-virgin olive oil

1 **cup** fresh corn kernels

1 **cup** chopped tomatoes (beautiful ones)

¼ **cup** torn fresh basil leaves

1 **tablespoon** freshly squeezed lemon juice

¼ **cup** thinly sliced scallions, white and light green parts only

---

Note: Flounder is a wonderful spring-to-summer fish, but it's delicate and prone to breaking when you remove it from the cooking bag. The solution is to take a sharp knife and cut the sides and top off the bag after removing it from the bath and then just lift the bag away. Then use a spatula to carefully move the fish to an oiled sheet pan for broiling. The broiling (in this case) will set the fish a bit more and just barely color it.

The corn, tomato, and basil in this recipe exudes summer simplicity. Flounder has a pure taste, clean and sublime, so I wanted to match it with seasonal produce that won't detract from its beauty but rather make it shine even more. When I say "fresh corn kernels" I mean you find fresh ears of beautiful corn and you cut those kernels off the cob. Also, when I say "beautiful tomato," you know what I mean. I mean a tomato you are proud of. There is no hiding subpar ingredients in a recipe this simple.

1. Preheat the circulator water bath to 51°C / 123.8°F.

2. Season the flounder fillets with ½ teaspoon of the kosher salt. Carefully place the flounder in a resealable gallon-size plastic bag and add the butter. Seal the bag using the displacement method (see page 17), and then immerse it in the circulator water bath. Cook for 15 minutes; after that, you can hold it there hot until you are ready to finish.

3. Remove the fish from the bag (using the cut-bag method described in the headnote) and let it cool for 2 to 3 minutes.

4. Meanwhile, heat the broiler on high. Grease a small sheet pan with 1 tablespoon of the olive oil.

5. Pat the fish dry with paper towels and transfer it to the prepared sheet tray. Broil for 3 minutes to help firm up the fish and get just a little bit of color.

6. While the fish is broiling, toss together the corn kernels, tomatoes, basil, lemon juice, and remaining ½ teaspoon salt in a medium bowl.

7. Once the fish is broiled to a golden hue, use a spatula to remove the fillets from the sheet tray and transfer them to a platter. Spoon the corn, tomato, and basil salad over the fish and scatter the sliced scallions on top. Serve.

46 SOUS VIDE

BACON-WRAPPED MONKFISH
with Cabbage and Potato Purée

Prep time: **25 minutes**

Cook time: **1¾ hours, plus 15 minutes finishing**

Circulator temperature setting: **85°C / 185°F for 45 minutes and then 53°C / 127.4°F for 1 hour**

SERVES 4

1 green cabbage, outer layers removed, cored, and chopped into ½-inch pieces (4 cups)

4 tablespoons (½ stick) cold unsalted butter, cubed

1 teaspoon freshly squeezed lemon juice

1½ teaspoons kosher salt

1 large monkfish fillet (1½ pounds)

4 to 8 thin slices bacon

2 cups Potato Purée (page 252)

1 tablespoon canola oil

¼ cup dry white vermouth

1 tablespoon whole-grain mustard

1 tablespoon minced fresh chives

This is a classic. It is a cold-weather dish to match with a red wine. Don't @ me about my choice of red wine with fish on this: It works. That old falsity of always white wine with fish is so limiting.

Monkfish is a beautifully textured firm fish, with an almost lobster-like richness. Most fish likes to rest a touch before being cut, and monkfish likes it more than most. Let it sit on the cutting board for five minutes after that final sear, and it will be a delightfully better meal.

As for the bacon in this recipe, I would get a butcher to thinly slice slab bacon because regular packaged sliced bacon is usually a touch too thick.

1. Preheat the circulator water bath to 85°C / 185°F.

2. Combine the cabbage, 2 tablespoons of the butter, the lemon juice, and ½ to ¾ teaspoon of the kosher salt in a large bowl and toss well to distribute the salt. Pack the cabbage into a resealable gallon-size plastic bag and seal it using the displacement method (see page 17). Immerse it in the circulator water bath. Cook for 45 minutes and then reduce the heat to 53°C / 127.4°F; keep the cabbage in the bath.

3. Cut the monkfish into 4 long cylinders, season them with the remaining ¾ teaspoon salt, and wrap a slice of bacon around each cylinder (use 2 if needed to fully cover them). Tightly roll each portion of monkfish in plastic wrap, tying off the ends with kitchen twine. Place the 4 portions in a resealable gallon-size plastic bag and seal it as above. Immerse it in the water bath (which should still have the cabbage hanging out to keep hot while you cook the fish). Cook the monkfish for 1 hour.

⫸➔ *Recipe continues*

4. Remove the bags from the hot water bath, and carefully unwrap each portion of monkfish. Set the fish on a cooling rack and let it rest for 5 minutes.

5. In a small saucepan set over medium-low heat, warm the potato purée.

6. Meanwhile, place a large skillet over medium heat, and when the skillet is hot, add the canola oil. Swirl the oil evenly around the pan and then add the monkfish portions, still wrapped in bacon, and cook, letting the bacon crisp up and rolling them over every minute or so, for a total of 5 minutes.

7. Transfer the fish to a cutting board and discard the oil from the skillet. Add the vermouth to the skillet and bring it to a boil. Turn off the heat but keep the pan on the burner. Add the mustard and whisk in the remaining 2 tablespoons butter. (If the sauce isn't smooth or looks greasy, add a small splash of water and whisk it all back together.) Remove the skillet from the heat and stir in the chives.

8. Divide each monkfish portion into 2 or 3 cuts. Remove the cabbage from the circulator. Arrange the monkfish on individual plates with the cabbage and the potato purée alongside, finishing each serving with a tablespoon or so of the mustard sauce.

TROUT

with Brown Butter Vinaigrette
and Fennel Slaw

Prep time: **30 minutes**

Cook time: **1 hour, plus
10 minutes finishing**

Circulator temperature
setting: **51°C / 123.8°F**

SERVES 4

1 tablespoon extra-virgin olive oil

2 shallots, sliced into thin rings

½ cup thinly sliced fennel bulb

Kosher salt

2 whole trout, cleaned, bones
removed, with fillets still connected
(1½ pounds total)

4 thin slices lemon

2 sprigs fresh thyme

3 tablespoons unsalted butter

2 tablespoons red wine vinegar

1 tablespoon freshly minced dill
fronds

Freshly ground black pepper

Fennel Slaw (recipe follows)

Trout with brown butter and fennel is like a camping trip in heaven, with Leonard Cohen and Amelia Earhart as your dinner companions. You can purchase whole trout and clean them yourself, or you can find butterflied fillets, still connected. The latter is what I used here, and it was a tasty treat.

The game plan is this: We will stuff the trout. Then we will truss the trout. Then we will sous vide the trout. Then we will broil the trout. Then we will eat the trout.

1. Preheat the circulator water bath to 51°C / 123.8°F.

2. Place a large skillet over medium heat. Add the olive oil, and once the oil shimmers, add the shallots and the fennel slices. Cook, stirring every minute or so, for about 5 minutes, until the shallots take on a little color and the fennel is really cooked down. Season with ½ teaspoon salt and stir to combine. Remove the skillet from the heat and transfer the shallot/fennel mixture to a small bowl to cool.

3. Arrange the butterflied trout on a sheet pan, skin-side down. Season them evenly on both sides with salt, and place them skin-side-down again. Place half of the shallot-fennel mixture on one side (one fillet) of each fish, and then top it with 2 lemon slices and a thyme sprig. Fold the other fillet over to encase the stuffing and then truss the trout with butcher's twine, making about 4 loops on each fish. Place the stuffed trout in a resealable gallon-size plastic bag and seal using the displacement method (see page 17). Submerge the bag in the circulator water bath and let the trout cook for 1 hour; after that, you can hold it there hot until you are ready to finish.

⟫→ *Recipe continues*

4. About 10 minutes before serving, preheat your broiler on high.

5. Let's make the brown butter: Place the butter in a small saucepan set over medium-high heat. Allow the butter to melt, swirling it occasionally in the pan, and continue cooking until the butter breaks into ghee and milk solids. After a couple of minutes, the milk solids will begin to brown, and this is good. You want that browning, because it gives the brown butter its characteristic nuttiness. When the milk solids have turned a deep brown, remove the pan from the heat and slowly drizzle in the vinegar. Add the minced dill and then season with salt and pepper to taste. Set aside.

6. Remove the bag from the hot water bath and transfer the trout to a paper towel. Dab them dry and use scissors to remove the kitchen twine. Place the trout on a clean sheet pan and broil for 2 to 3 minutes, until nicely browned. Carefully turn them over with a spatula and broil for 2 to 3 minutes more. Remove the trout from the broiler and transfer them to a platter. Drizzle with the brown butter and serve with the fennel slaw.

FENNEL SLAW

Makes 2 cups

I baseball-size fennel bulb

¼ cup shaved red onion

2 tablespoons chopped fresh dill fronds

½ teaspoon kosher salt

Juice of I lemon

2 tablespoons extra-virgin olive oil

Core the fennel bulb and slice it thinly against the grain. Toss the fennel in a small bowl with the red onion, dill, and salt. Add the lemon juice and olive oil, and let sit at room temperature for 1 hour. Leftover slaw will keep in the refrigerator for 3 days.

LOBSTER ROLLS

Prep time: **30 minutes**

Cook time: **1 hour, plus 15 minutes finishing**

Circulator temperature setting: **54°C / 129.2°F**

S E R V E S 4

3 lobsters (1½ pounds each)

Kosher salt

1½ tablespoons fresh tarragon leaves, chopped

5 tablespoons cold unsalted butter, cubed

½ **cup** mayonnaise

½ shallot, minced

2 tablespoons diced celery

1 tablespoon thinly sliced fresh chives

2 tablespoons freshly squeezed lemon juice

Fine sea salt

4 hot dog rolls (I like potato rolls)

2 tablespoons celery leaves, chopped

These are Maine-style lobster salad rolls. They are a simple yet decadent treat. If you are from Connecticut, and prefer the style of just hot lobster with drawn butter, then you should block this recipe from your mind so you don't debate yourself over the merits of your style. Yes, we know you don't use mayo and that you serve it warm. We hear you. This is a Maine-style lobster roll.

1. Preheat the circulator water bath to 54°C / 129.2°F.

2. (Humanely) kill the lobsters by using a knife to split the heads in half: Insert the tip of a sharp chef's knife straight down into the body right below the head, then firmly come down on the head with the blade to split it. Next, carefully twist off the tails and cut away the claws. With the shells still on, insert two wooden or metal skewers into each tail. This will make sure the tails lie flat while they cook.

3. Bring a large pot of heavily salted water to a boil. Set up an ice bath. Once the water has reached a boil, carefully add the tails and claws and cook for 1 minute. Using tongs, gently remove the tails and claws from the boiling water and immediately plunge them into the ice bath. Once the lobster meat is cool, remove the meat from tails, claws, and knuckles.

4. Cut the lobster meat into bite-size (1-inch) pieces. Place the cut-up lobster meat, 1 tablespoon of the tarragon, and 3 tablespoons of the butter into a resealable gallon-size plastic bag. Season with a few pinches of kosher salt. Use the displacement method (see page 17) to seal the bag. Submerge it into the circulator water bath and cook for 1 hour.

⋙✦ *Recipe continues*

5. Remove the bag from the hot water bath and drain off the liquid, reserving the lobster meat. Transfer the meat to a medium bowl and let it cool in the fridge for 10 minutes.

6. Remove the bowl from the fridge and add the remaining ½ tablespoon tarragon along with the mayonnaise, shallot, diced celery, chives, and lemon juice and mix gently until the lobster is well covered. Season with sea salt to taste.

7. To toast the potato rolls, place a large skillet over medium high-heat and add the remaining 2 tablespoons butter. Once the butter begins to froth, add the rolls and toast for about 2 minutes on each side, until golden brown.

8. To serve, place the toasted rolls on a serving platter and spoon an equal amount of the lobster mixture onto each roll. Garnish with the celery leaves. Enjoy!

SQUID

Stuffed with Chickpeas, Swiss Chard, and Garlic

Prep time: **30 minutes**

Cook time: **1 hour, plus 5 minutes finishing**

Circulator temperature setting: **60°C / 140°F**

SERVES 4

- **2 tablespoons** olive oil, plus more for brushing the squid
- **4 cups** stemmed and coarsely chopped Swiss chard
- **2** garlic cloves, minced
- **2 cups** cooked chickpeas (canned are fine)
- **1 teaspoon** ground cumin
- **2 teaspoons** smoked paprika
- **Pinch** of cayenne pepper
- **2 teaspoons** freshly squeezed lemon juice
- Kosher salt and freshly ground black pepper
- **2 pounds** squid tubes and tentacles, rinsed, clear sheath removed from tubes and beak removed
- **½ to 1** serrano chile, very thinly sliced
- **2 tablespoons** minced fresh flat-leaf parsley leaves

I finished these wonderful squid on a grill, but you can finish them in a pan if you feel less inclined to light up the fire for a pretty short grill time. Grill pans are cool should you have one, or just a quick sear in a cast-iron skillet will do the trick. Any which way, really, but do make the dish, because it is delicious—the savory, earthy stuffing of greens and chickpeas balances the sweetness of the seared squid. If you can find fresh squid, buy it, but frozen is fine as well.

When cleaning squid, there is a clear bonelike quill in the body that needs to be removed, and then a beak in the center of the tentacle structure that should also be popped out. Your fishmonger may have already done this for you; if not, it's not hard to find these things and just get 'em out yourself.

1. Preheat the circulator water bath to 60°C / 140°F.

2. Add 1 tablespoon of the oil to a large skillet set over medium-high heat. When the oil begins to shimmer, add the Swiss chard and cook for 2 minutes. Add the garlic and cook for 1 minute more, until the chard has wilted well. Transfer the chard to a plate lined with a paper towel and let it cool.

3. In a small food processor, pulse the chickpeas to form a rough mash. Mince the chard with a knife and fold it into the chickpeas. Add the cumin, 1 teaspoon of the paprika, the cayenne, 1 tablespoon of the oil, and the lemon juice. Pulse and season with salt and pepper to taste.

4. Season the squid with salt and stuff the tubes with the chickpea-chard mixture, making sure to not overstuff them. Carefully place the stuffed tubes and the tentacles in a resealable gallon-size plastic bag and seal it using the displacement method (see page 17). Submerge the bag in the circulator water bath and cook the squid for 1 hour; after that, you can hold it there hot until you are ready to finish.

》→ *Recipe continues*

5. While the squid is cooking, light your grill and get it up to medium-high heat. (Alternatively, you could heat a grill pan or cast-iron skillet over medium-high heat.)

6. When the squid is done, remove the bag from the hot water bath and transfer the squid to a plate lined with paper towels. Pat it dry.

7. Brush the squid with a little olive oil and arrange the tubes on the grill. Cook for 2 to 3 minutes—you're just looking to get some nice grill marks and some char; don't overcook or the squid will become chewy. Add the tentacles and cook them for 1 minute (tentacles don't take as long to cook as tubes, but be vigilant and try to keep them from falling into the grill). Transfer the squid to a platter. You can leave the tubes whole or cut them into thick slices.

8. Serve, garnished with the serrano slices and parsley. Sprinkle the remaining 1 teaspoon of the smoked paprika over the top.

GARLIC BUTTER SHRIMP
on Toast

Prep time: **20 minutes**

Cook time: **30 minutes**

Circulator temperature
setting: **57°C / 134.6°F**

SERVES 4

1 pound large shrimp
(21 to 25 shrimp),
peeled and deveined

¼ cup (½ stick) unsalted butter,
plus 2 tablespoons at room
temperature

3 garlic cloves, minced

1½ teaspoons kosher salt

Pinch of crushed red pepper flakes

2 tablespoons freshly grated
lemon zest

4 slices of your favorite bread

1 tablespoon fresh flat-leaf
parsley leaves

1 tablespoon celery leaves
(pale green leaves only)

Freshly minced chives, for serving

4 lemon wedges, for serving

I really like garlicky things on toast. Toast just soaks up the goodness, and the results are delightful. Add some beautiful shrimp, a hint of lemon and red pepper flakes, the cool crispness of celery, and you have a recipe that can be an anchor for many summer meals, which is the time to buy fresh American shrimp.

1. Preheat the circulator water bath to 57°C / 134.6°F.

2. In a resealable gallon-size plastic bag, combine the shrimp, ¼ cup butter, the garlic, salt, red pepper flakes, and lemon zest. Seal the bag using the displacement method (see page 17). Submerge the bag in the circulator water bath and cook for 30 minutes; after that, you can hold it there hot until you are ready to finish.

3. Five minutes before serving, brush the sliced bread with the remaining 2 tablespoons butter and toast it to your liking.

4. Remove the bag from the hot water bath and pour the contents into a large mixing bowl. Place the toast on a platter and evenly divide the shrimp among the slices. (Be sure to get all that melted butter and garlic to spoon on top as well.) Garnish with the parsley, celery leaves, and chives, and finish with a squeeze of lemon over each toast. Eat.

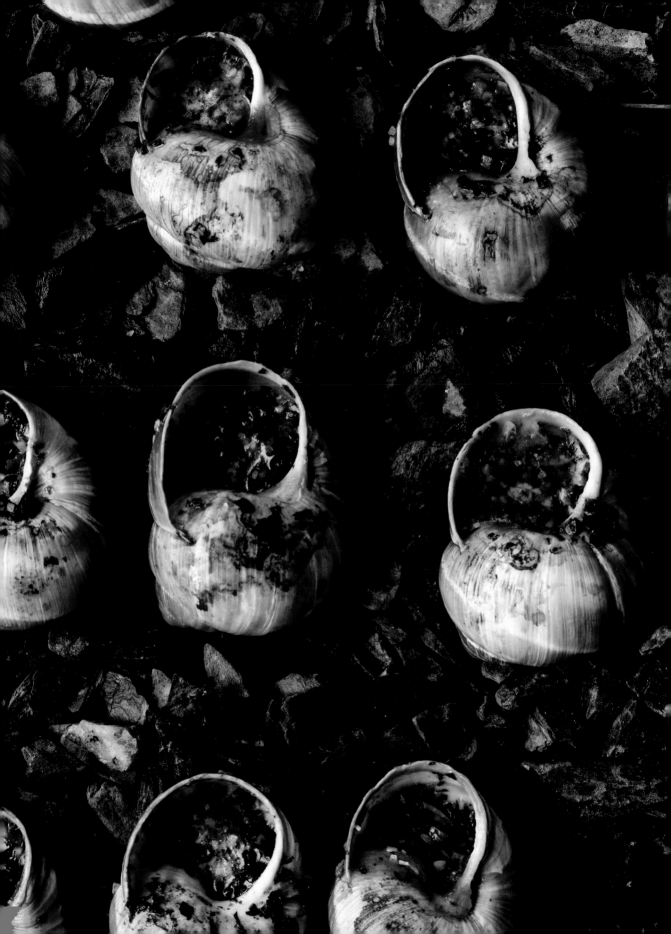

SNAILS

with Garlic Butter and Parsley

Prep time: **10 minutes**

Cook time: **1 hour,
plus 25 minutes finishing**

Circulator temperature
setting: **54°C / 129.2°F**

SERVES 4

24 canned escargots

2 cups dashi (page 193)

1 tablespoon light soy sauce

1 cup (2 sticks) unsalted butter,
at room temperature

½ **cup** minced fresh flat-leaf parsley
leaves

2 shallots, minced

2 tablespoons cognac

4 garlic cloves, minced

Fine sea salt and freshly ground black
pepper

24 escargot shells (optional; see Note)

Toast, for serving

I do love me some snails. This version is the ubiquitous Burgundian staple that you see in cafés all over France. They are buttery and lovely and saline, with a little tender bite.

Before you say, "I can't get snails in my town," realize that I get mine sent to my door, from a huge company that offers free shipping. I am all for supporting local businesses, but really no one has a local snail shop in Athens, Georgia. So I buy cans of them, the ones labeled with the species *Helix lucorum*. Search "escargots," because a search for "snails" results in some gardening critters, but "escargots" leads you to culinary offerings. These are the tasty little gray snails of Burgundy, where you will find escargots on pretty much every menu. This is my version of that classic—the sweet snails are loaded with a subtle umami boost from dashi and soy sauce.

1. Preheat the circulator bath to 54°C / 129.2°F

2. Drain the snails from the can and rinse them under cold water. Place the snails in a resealable gallon-size plastic bag and add the dashi and soy sauce. Seal the bag with the displacement method (see page 17). Immerse the bag in the circulator bath and cook for 1 hour; after that, you can hold it there hot until you're ready to finish.

3. While the snails are cooking, make the garlic butter: Place the butter, parsley, shallots, cognac, and garlic in a food processor and process until smooth. Add salt and pepper to taste and pulse once more to evenly season the mixture. Scoop the garlic butter into a bowl and set aside.

⟫→ *Recipe continues*

Note: If you don't have escargot shells or an escargot pan, simply arrange the snails in a baking dish, with an inch of space around each one, and spread the garlic butter over the snails before baking them.

4. When you are ready to serve the escargots, preheat the oven to 400°F. Fill a shallow baking dish or rimmed sheet pan with a layer of dried beans or rock salt to keep the shells from rolling around (see Note).

5. Transfer the garlic butter to a small plastic bag, snip off the corner to make a piping bag, and then fill each escargot shell with garlic butter.

6. Remove the snails from the bag and drain them, discarding the poaching liquid. Place one snail in each butter-filled shell and push it to the bottom. Arrange the shells on the prepared baking dish and bake in the oven for 15 minutes, until piping hot. Serve with some of your favorite bread, well-toasted.

CHARRED OCTOPUS

with Orange, Cured Olives, Frisée, and Mint Vinaigrette

Prep time: **15 minutes**

Cook time: **6 hours, plus 20 minutes finishing**

Circulator temperature setting: **75°C / 167°F**

SERVES 4

1 octopus (about 2 pounds), head removed above the eyes

1½ **teaspoons** kosher salt

1 **tablespoon** chopped fresh thyme leaves

1 **teaspoon** ground Espelette chile

Freshly ground black pepper

½ **teaspoon** freshly ground coriander seeds

¾ **cup** extra-virgin olive oil

1 **tablespoon** Dijon mustard

2 **tablespoons** red wine vinegar

3 **tablespoons** minced fresh mint leaves

1 **tablespoon** canola oil

2 **cups** frisée, torn into bite-size pieces

¼ **cup** oil-cured black olives, pitted and sliced

1 **cup** freshly cut orange supremes (see page 29)

If you told me ten years ago that octopus would be on virtually every contemporary cheffy American menu, I would have said you were going crazy, but here we are. I think the popularity of Spanish and Portuguese food helped the tentacles reach new menus, and the results are pretty awesome. Be aware of where your octopus is from, though, as with popularity comes a waning of supply through vast overfishing. The best choice we have is pot-caught from various places around the globe, such as the waters around Alaska, Hawaii, and Spain. Pot-caught is precise and doesn't result in a lot of by-catch, a horribly common result of bottom-trawl fishing.

This dish is an homage to the flavors of North Africa and Andalusia in Spain, two cuisines that are brothers from another mother. Get good oil-cured black olives with their bright, pungent, briny flavors. Oil-cured olives aren't really cured in olive oil, but rather are salted and cured first, and then bathed in oil to marinate and store them (often with the addition of citrus and herbs). You see them in Morocco a lot, but they can be found pretty much wherever you look, or online in a pinch.

1. Preheat the circulator water bath to 75°C / 167°F.

2. Rinse the octopus under cold water. Turn it over and you will see the beak, which is kind of like a hard, round bone, in the center of the underside. Use a paring knife to cut it out and discard it. Cut away the eyes and discard them, then separate the tentacles. You should have 8 tentacles, unless someone sold you an octopus with 6 arms. If this has happened, you should find a new fishmonger.

3. Season the octopus with 1 teaspoon of the salt, the thyme, Espelette chile, black pepper, and coriander. Place

⋙→ *Recipe continues*

the octopus in a resealable gallon-size plastic bag and add ¼ cup of the olive oil. Seal it using the displacement method (see page 17). Immerse the bag in the circulator water bath. Cook for 6 hours, until the octopus is very tender; after that, you can hold it there hot until you are ready to finish.

4. Five minutes before you remove the octopus from the water, set up an ice bath.

5. Remove the bag from the hot water bath and submerge it in the ice bath for 15 minutes, until cool.

6. Meanwhile, make the vinaigrette: Place the mustard and red wine vinegar in a blender and combine on low speed. With the blender running, slowly drizzle in the remaining ½ cup oil, remaining ½ teaspoon salt, and the mint through the opening in the lid, and blend until smooth. Turn off the blender and pour the vinaigrette into a small jar.

7. Remove the octopus from the chilled bag, discard any liquid, and pat the octopus dry with paper towels.

8. Heat a cast-iron skillet over high heat. Add the canola oil, and when the oil comes to a light smoke, add the octopus. Cook for 4 minutes per side, or until the skin is nice and charred. Transfer the octopus to a cutting board and slice it into more manageable pieces for serving, or leave the tentacles whole if you prefer.

9. In a medium bowl, combine the octopus with the frisée, olives, and orange supreme. Add the vinaigrette to your liking and toss gently. Plate it up.

BIRDS
(& EGGS)

Which came first is not the priority here. You will be asking why haven't you crossed the sous vide road with the chicken very soon, though, because cooking chicken, fowl, and eggs in a sous vide setup is simple and delicious.

This chapter doesn't stop with chicken. It shows you the ease and wonder of cooking a lot of our flying fowl, like guinea hen, quail, and duck. The duck confit recipe is arguably the best use of sous vide ever, because you can use a trace amount of the duck fat that is called for in most confit recipes and still get unctuous results.

We will go through several different styles of cooking in this chapter, from brawny stews to pretty roasts, from stuffed little birds to classic breast presentations, exploring the many nuances of cooking those birds with the confidence that they'll be just-cooked and juicy.

CHICKEN WINGS
with Celery Salad

Prep time: **6 hours brining, plus 30 minutes prep**

Cook time: **1½ hours, plus 10 minutes finishing**

Circulator temperature setting: **64°C / 147.2°F**

SERVES 4

24 Brined Chicken Wings (recipe follows)

Kosher salt and freshly ground black pepper

5 celery stalks, peeled and sliced on the diagonal into ¼-inch-thick pieces

¼ **cup** thinly sliced shallots (about 2 shallots)

¼ **cup** fresh parsley leaves, chopped

¼ **cup** shaved Parmesan cheese

3 tablespoons freshly squeezed lemon juice

¼ **cup** extra-virgin olive oil

½ **cup** Hot Wing Sauce (recipe follows)

1½ **cups** Ranch Dressing (recipe follows), for serving

Mastery of chicken wings means gaining friends because most humans love chicken wings. These are classics in the Buffalo style, spicy and buttery, and perfectly cooked. Pack them up in a foil pack and bring them to the football game. Tailgaters will love you. The ranch dressing recipe here is a gem outside of the realm of Hidden Valley, and the celery salad classes up the party.

1. Preheat the circulator water bath to 64°C / 147.2°F.

2. Remove those chicken wings from the brine and season them well with salt and pepper. Place the chicken wings in a resealable gallon-size plastic bag and seal using the displacement method (see page 17). Submerge the bag in the circulator water bath and cook for 1½ hours; after that, you can hold it there hot until you are ready to finish.

3. Set your oven broiler on high and line a broiler-safe pan with aluminum foil.

4. When the chicken is done, remove the bag from the water bath and transfer the chicken wings to the foil-lined pan, arranging them in an even layer. Discard the liquid in the bag. Broil the wings, flipping them over once, until they are brown and crisp on both sides, about 10 minutes total.

5. While the wings are under the broiler, make the celery salad: In a medium bowl, combine the celery, shallots, parsley, and Parmesan. Season with salt and pepper to taste, and add the lemon juice and olive oil. Toss well to combine and set aside.

6. Remove the wings from the broiler and transfer them to a medium bowl. Add the hot wing sauce and toss to evenly coat. Serve the wings immediately, with the celery salad on the side and the ranch dressing for dipping, or let them cool and pack 'em to go. Set out extra napkins, too. It's messy.

BRINED CHICKEN WINGS

Makes 24 wings

If you make this brine ahead, it will keep in the fridge for 2 weeks. This will make plenty of brine for this one recipe, so you'll have some extra.

1 cup (about 200 grams) Diamond Crystal kosher salt

¼ cup sugar

1 tablespoon whole black peppercorns

½ tablespoon allspice berries

3 sprigs fresh thyme

24 bone-in, skin-on chicken wings

Combine the salt, sugar, peppercorns, allspice berries, and thyme sprigs in a stockpot. Add 1 gallon water and bring to a boil over high heat. Cook, stirring occasionally, until the salt and sugar are dissolved. Remove the brine from the heat and let it cool to room temperature.

Transfer the brine to a large nonreactive container. (A large Pyrex container or three or four resealable gallon-size plastic bags will work well, but if you use plastic bags for the brine, be sure to put them into bowls in case a bag breaks.) Add the chicken wings to the brining solution, making sure they are fully immersed. Cover and refrigerate for 6 hours or overnight.

HOT WING SAUCE

Makes ½ cup

Simple hot sauce comes easy. This is still easy but better. Butter, hot sauce, and a stove. You can do this.

¼ cup (½ stick) unsalted butter

¼ cup hot sauce (I like Cholula hot sauce)

In a small saucepan set over medium high heat, combine the butter and hot sauce and cook, whisking, until the butter has fully melted and has been incorporated into the hot sauce. Use immediately; if you chill it, you'll have to cook and whisk it back together.

RANCH DRESSING

Makes 1½ cups

Making your own ranch dressing is one step closer to removing an entire aisle from your trip to the grocery store. You can use that crème fraîche you made earlier, too. So thrifty.

¼ cup mayonnaise

½ cup buttermilk

½ cup crème fraîche (page 195) or sour cream

1 tablespoon freshly squeezed lemon juice

1 teaspoon cider vinegar

1 tablespoon finely minced fresh chives

1 teaspoon minced fresh dill fronds

½ teaspoon garlic powder

¼ teaspoon kosher salt

1 teaspoon hot sauce

In a small bowl, combine the mayonnaise, buttermilk, crème fraîche, lemon juice, cider vinegar, chives, dill, garlic powder, salt, and hot sauce. Whisk well to combine. The ranch dressing will stay fresh, covered, for a week in the fridge.

QUAILS
with Chorizo and Cornbread Stuffing

Prep time: **30 minutes**

Cook time: **1½ hours, plus 10 minutes finishing**

Circulator temperature setting: **64°C / 147.2°F**

SERVES 4

- **1 tablespoon** extra-virgin olive oil
- 1 shallot, minced
- **½ pound** Mexican chorizo, casing removed
- **1 cup** diced Cornbread (recipe follows)
- **1 tablespoon** dried Mexican oregano
- **2 tablespoons** chopped fresh epazote
- **2 tablespoons** chicken stock (page 188)
- **2 teaspoons** kosher salt
- 4 euro-boneless quails

This recipe has a couple of steps to it, but the final stage is so easy that it makes for a great crowd-pleaser, and you don't have to work up a sweat at the actual party. First, we will make some cornbread; second, we will make a stuffing with cooked Mexican chorizo and the cornbread; third, we will stuff the quails and wrap them up good and tight in plastic wrap; and then we'll cook them and finally broil them to a crisp skin once they are finished with their bath.

You could serve these as a part of a larger meal, but it is wonderful as a single course with a simple salad of tomatoes, avocado, and shaved white onion.

Epazote is an herb commonly found in Mexican food—often in bean dishes because on top of boasting a heady flavor it is thought to reduce farting. Though that is interesting, it does really have a nice flavor, almost like fennel seed mixed with oregano and spruce. If you can't find it fresh, you can usually get it dried. Look for it at Mexican groceries.

"Euro-boneless" means quails that have been deboned except for the wing and leg bones. When stuffed they look like tiny turduckens.

1. Preheat the circulator water bath to 64°C / 147.2°F.

2. Place a large skillet over medium heat and add the olive oil. When the oil shimmers, add the shallot and cook for 1 minute. Add the chorizo and crush it down with a wooden spoon. Cook, stirring occasionally, until it is cooked through and browned, about 8 minutes. Strain the mixture to get rid of any residual fat. Discard the fat and transfer the chorizo to a bowl. Lightly crumble the cornbread into the chorizo, and add the oregano and epazote. Add the chicken stock to moisten the mixture, and season with 1 teaspoon of the salt. Mix well and set aside.

≫→ *Recipe continues*

3. Rinse the quails under cold water and pat them dry. Lay them on a cutting board and then stuff each one with about ¼ cup of the stuffing. Season them all over with the remaining 1 teaspoon salt. Wrap each one tightly in plastic wrap and place them in a resealable gallon-size plastic bag; seal the bag with the displacement method (see page 17). Immerse the bag in the circulator water bath and cook for 1½ hours; after that, you can hold it there hot until you're ready to finish.

4. Ten minutes before you are ready to finish the quail, preheat the broiler to high.

5. Remove the quails from the water bath, unwrap each one from its plastic wrap, and place them on paper towels to blot away any excess liquid. Arrange the quails in a broiler-safe pan and broil until golden brown, 3 to 4 minutes.

6. Remove the quails from the oven and let them rest for a couple of minutes. Cut each quail in half and present them on a platter.

CORNBREAD
Makes one 10-inch skillet's-worth

2 cups white cornmeal

½ cup all-purpose flour

1 teaspoon baking powder

1 teaspoon baking soda

½ teaspoon kosher salt

¾ cup whole milk

¾ cup buttermilk

1 large egg

¼ cup bacon fat

Preheat the oven to 425°F.

In a large bowl, combine the cornmeal, flour, baking powder, baking soda, and salt and stir.

In a separate bowl, combine the milk, buttermilk, and egg and beat with a whisk until the egg is incorporated. Add this wet mix to the dry mixture. Stir well to combine.

Heat a 10-inch cast-iron skillet over medium heat and add the bacon fat. When the fat and the pan are hot, add the hot fat to the batter and stir. Pour the batter into the cast-iron skillet and bake for 20 minutes, or until a toothpick inserted into the center comes out clean.

Remove the cornbread from the oven and let it cool in the skillet. Once it is cool enough to handle, carefully flip the skillet over, releasing the cornbread onto a cutting board (if it doesn't want to come out cleanly, run a paring knife around the edge of the skillet). Let the cornbread cool completely. You can always make the cornbread in advance and freeze it in a zip-lock bag.

CHICKEN THIGHS

with Romesco Yogurt Sauce, Shaved
Manchego, and Charred Onion

Prep time: **20 minutes**

Cook time: **4 hours, plus
30 minutes to finish**

Circulator temperature
setting: **74°C / 165.2°F**

SERVES 4

4 bone-in, skin-on chicken thighs

Kosher salt and freshly ground black
pepper

2 sprigs fresh thyme

2 garlic cloves

⅔ **cup** skin-on unsalted almonds,
toasted

½ **cup** chopped roasted red bell
peppers (see Note, page 80)

1 Roma tomato, seeded and diced

½ **teaspoon** smoked paprika

1 tablespoon sherry vinegar

4 tablespoons olive oil

2 tablespoons plain yogurt

1 large sweet yellow or red onion,
sliced into ½-inch-thick rounds

½ **cup** shaved Manchego cheese

1 tablespoon minced fresh mint
leaves, for garnish

1 tablespoon minced fresh cilantro
leaves, for garnish

Sous vide chicken thighs are one of the best things to have around in the fridge. You can have them completely done except for the final crisping in a pan—and that means you have an efficient dinner at your fingertips at any time. Remember, it still counts as cooking from scratch even if you prepped most of the meal a few days ago.

Romesco is the roasted pepper sauce of Spain. It is a beautiful symphony of pulverized garlic, smoked paprika, almonds, and sweet smoky capsicums. It should be a staple in your arsenal of food. You can use it straight-up in pretty much anything, but here we blend in some yogurt for a smooth sauce.

1. Preheat the circulator water bath to 74°C / 165.2°F.

2. Season the chicken thighs well with salt and pepper. In a resealable gallon-size plastic bag, combine the thighs, thyme sprigs, and 1 garlic clove. Seal the bag using the displacement method (see page 17). Submerge the bag in the hot water bath and cook for 4 hours; after that, you can hold it there hot until you're ready to finish.

3. Meanwhile, make the romesco: In a blender, combine the remaining garlic clove, ⅓ cup of the almonds, the roasted red peppers, tomato, paprika, and sherry vinegar. Pulse a few times, until the mixture is just beginning to turn smooth. Then turn the blender to low and drizzle in 2 tablespoons of the olive oil. This is romesco. Congratulations!

4. To finish the sauce, add the yogurt to the romesco and season it with a pinch of salt. Continue to blend on low speed for 30 seconds or until the sauce is smooth. Set aside.

⫸ *Recipe continues*

Note: Roasting peppers is often done without much care and this makes me very sad. A common method is to plop them in a hot oven for 30 minutes. But then they cook too much, reducing the flesh to a purée. Success is had with a shorter cooking time. Putting them right on a gas burner, turning them with tongs as soon as one side is blackened, is a great way to accomplish this, but nothing rivals a super-hot grill. When they are done blackening, seal them up in a plastic freezer bag—this will help steam off the skins. Wipe away the skins, rinsing the peppers a touch if needed. Break them open and cut out the seed structure and stem.

5. Coarsely chop the remaining ⅓ cup toasted almonds and set aside.

6. Remove the chicken thighs from the bag and discard the thyme and garlic. Place the thighs skin-side down between paper towels to dry the skin.

7. In a large cast-iron skillet, heat the remaining 2 tablespoons olive oil over medium-high heat. When the oil begins to shimmer, add the chicken thighs skin-side down. Press down firmly on the thighs with a spatula or spoon to make sure there is even contact between the skin and the skillet, and cook the chicken until the skin is dark brown and crispy, about 5 minutes. Using a pair of tongs, turn the chicken over and cook on the other side for 2 minutes, or until browned. Remove the chicken from the skillet and transfer it to a plate lined with a paper towel to rest.

8. Return the same cast-iron skillet to the stove and raise the heat to high. Add the onion rounds and season them with salt and pepper. Cook the onion rounds on one side until well charred, 4 to 5 minutes. Using a spatula, transfer the onions to a plate to cool. When they are cool enough to handle, separate them into individual rings.

9. To serve, arrange the chicken thighs on a large plate. Top the chicken with a few spoonfuls of romesco, and then place the rings of charred onion around the chicken. Garnish with the shaved Manchego, reserved chopped almonds, mint, and cilantro. Eat!

POLLO CRIOLLO

(Cuban Mojo Chicken)

Prep time: **20 minutes**

Cook time: **2 hours, plus 10 minutes finishing**

Circulator temperature setting: **68°C / 154.4°F**

SERVES 4

8 garlic cloves, minced

1 **teaspoon** fresh oregano leaves

¼ **teaspoon** ground nutmeg

1 **teaspoon** cumin seeds, toasted

Kosher salt

1 **cup** freshly squeezed orange juice

¼ **cup** freshly squeezed lime juice

¼ **cup** extra-virgin olive oil

½ **cup** dry white wine

1 **cup** fresh cilantro leaves and stems, minced

1 whole chicken (about 4 pounds), backbone removed, cut into 8 pieces

2 **tablespoons** unsalted butter

1 medium sweet onion (like Vidalia or Maui), thinly sliced

This is a Cuban staple that melds a wonderfully simple mojo—a citrus-garlic sauce—with plump chicken and lots of sweet onions. The key is to let it broil for a while at the end, resulting in nicely crisped skin and almost caramelized onions. Serve it up with some rice and beans and a cold beer.

1. Preheat the circulator water bath to 68°C / 154.4°F.

2. In a blender, combine the garlic, oregano, nutmeg, cumin seeds, 1 teaspoon kosher salt, orange juice, lime juice, olive oil, white wine, and cilantro and purée until smooth. Season with more salt to taste.

3. Season the chicken parts with 1 tablespoon kosher salt. Place the chicken in a resealable gallon-size plastic bag and add the marinade from the blender. Seal the bag with the displacement method (see page 17), submerge it in the water bath, and cook for 2 hours; after that, you can hold it there hot until you're ready to finish.

4. Fifteen minutes before you're ready to finish the dish, place a 12-inch broiler-safe skillet over medium heat. Add the butter, and when it begins to froth, add the onion. Cook for 15 minutes, stirring occasionally, until the onion is translucent and evenly caramelized. Remove the skillet from the heat and set it aside.

5. Heat the broiler to high. Remove the bag from the water bath and carefully pour the chicken, sauce and all, over the onions in the skillet. Place the skillet on an oven rack just above the center of the oven and broil for 10 minutes, watching it closely, until the chicken skin is all bubbling and brown. (If your oven has the broiler in a small shelf under the oven, broil the chicken under a low flame until browned.) Serve.

PRESSED CRISP CHICKEN THIGHS

with Red Curry, Coconut, Thai Basil, and Avocado

Prep time: **30 minutes**

Cook time: **1 hour, plus 45 minutes finishing**

Circulator temperature setting: **65°C / 149°F**

SERVES 4

- **4** large bone-in, skin-on chicken thighs
- **2 teaspoons** kosher salt
- **1 tablespoon** canola oil
- **1** shallot, minced
- **2 tablespoons** minced celery
- **1 tablespoon** minced fresh ginger
- **1 tablespoon** minced tender lemongrass (see Note, page 33)
- **2 tablespoons** Thai red curry paste
- **1 cup** chicken stock (page 188)
- **1 cup** unsweetened coconut milk
- **1** ripe avocado, peeled, pitted, and sliced into ½-inch-thick half-moons
- **¼ cup** fresh Thai basil leaves
- Lime wedges, for serving

These chicken thighs crisp up to a golden goodness with the last step in a skillet. The simple coconut curry is punchy and bright, a basic but delicious way of showing off some of the flavors of Thai food.

1. Preheat the circulator water bath to 65°C / 149°F.

2. Trim the excess fat from the chicken thighs and season them all over with 1 teaspoon of the kosher salt. Place the thighs in a resealable gallon-size plastic bag and seal with the displacement method (page 17). Submerge the bag in the circulator water bath and cook for 1 hour; after that, you can hold it there hot until you're ready to finish. (If you want to cool the chicken and finish it later, you can shock the bag in ice water and then keep it in the fridge; but for a cleaner, less jelly-covered result, you can remove the bag from the bath and transfer the chicken to a cooling rack set over a sheet pan. Discard the cooking liquids from the bag and let the chicken chill in the fridge for 2 hours.)

3. Transfer the chicken to a cutting board. Using a paring knife, cut around the bone in each thigh and pull it out. Trim away any remaining connective tissue that looks like it would be a wrestle to chew. Flip the thighs so that they are skin-side up, and using a heavy flat-bottomed pan, press down on each thigh to flatten it to a uniform thickness of about 1 inch. Pat the skin side dry with paper towels.

4. Heat the canola oil in a large skillet set over medium heat. When the oil begins to shimmer, add the chicken, skin-side down, and cook until the skin is very golden and crisp, about 10 minutes. Remove the chicken from the skillet and set it aside on a plate.

5. Add the shallot, celery, ginger, and lemongrass to the skillet and cook about 5 minutes, until the vegetables are well sweated down and just beginning to color. Stir in the curry paste and the chicken stock, and cook 5 minutes more to marry the flavors and reduce the stock. Then stir in the coconut milk and return the chicken thighs to the skillet, skin-side up to keep it dry. Add the avocado and cook for 1 minute, until it is just warmed through. Season with the remaining 1 teaspoon salt.

6. To serve, ladle some of the sauce into individual serving bowls. Add a chicken thigh to each bowl, and ladle additional sauce over the chicken. Arrange fresh basil on top, and garnish with lime wedges.

NASHVILLE HOT CHICKEN

Prep time: **24 hours in fridge**

Cook time: **1½ hours, plus 30 minutes finishing**

Circulator temperature setting: **70°C / 158°F**

SERVES 4

- **4** chicken leg quarters
- **1 tablespoon plus ½ teaspoon** kosher salt
- **2 cups** buttermilk
- **½ cup** (1 stick) unsalted butter
- **1 tablespoon** cayenne pepper
- **1 tablespoon** pimentón dulce (see Note, page 25)
- **1 teaspoon** light brown sugar
- **½ teaspoon** garlic salt
- **½ teaspoon** freshly ground black pepper
- **2 cups** vegetable oil
- **2 cups** lard
- **2 cups** all-purpose flour
- Bread-and-Butter Pickles (page 208), for serving
- **4 to 6 slices** white bread, for serving

Um, I have to be honest: I love spicy food, I really do. But some Nashville hot fried chicken is just too much. This version imparts a kick for rational taste buds. It is a two-step recipe, but since the chicken is already beautifully cooked before you fry it, the frying is fast and consistent.

1. Arrange the chicken leg quarters in a single layer, skin-side up, on a sheet pan or in a baking dish. Salt the skin side evenly with 1 tablespoon kosher salt. Refrigerate, uncovered, for 24 hours.

2. Preheat the circulator water bath to 70°C / 158°F.

3. Remove the chicken from the fridge and pat it dry with a paper towel. Place the chicken in a resealable gallon-size plastic bag and seal the bag using the displacement method (page 17). Submerge the bag in the circulator water bath and cook for 1½ hours; after that, you can hold it there hot until you're ready to finish.

4. Remove the chicken from the plastic bag. Pour the buttermilk into a large bowl. Add the chicken quarters to the buttermilk and turn to coat. Set aside.

5. In a small saucepan set over medium-high heat, melt the butter. When it begins to bubble, add the cayenne, pimentón, brown sugar, garlic salt, black pepper, and remaining ½ teaspoon kosher salt. Cook, stirring frequently, for 2 minutes to infuse the flavors. Remove the pan from the heat and leave the spiced butter on the stove to keep it at an ambient warm temperature.

6. Place a large deep cast-iron skillet or Dutch oven over medium-high heat and add the vegetable oil and lard. Set a wire cooling rack over a sheet pan, and place it near the stove. Bring the frying oil mix up to 375°F (190.6°C).

⫸→ *Recipe continues*

7. While the oil is heating, pour the flour into a large paper bag. Remove the chicken legs, one at a time, from the buttermilk, letting the excess liquid drip back into the bowl, and add the chicken to the paper bag. When all the legs are in the bag, fold the top down a couple of times and shake the bag to coat the chicken with the flour. Remove the chicken legs and shake off any excess flour.

8. Carefully add the chicken to the frying oil, skin-side down. Cook for 3 minutes per side, or until the skin is golden and crispy. Using a pair of tongs, remove the chicken from the oil and transfer them to the cooling rack. While the chicken is resting for 5 minutes, brush each leg heavily with the spice butter.

9. Serve the chicken with a ton of bread-and-butter pickles and some white bread. The more basic the setup, the better.

GUINEA HEN PIBIL TACOS

Prep time: **30 minutes**

Cook time: **I hour, plus 10 minutes finishing**

Circulator temperature setting: **71°C / 159.8°F**

SERVES 4

1 guinea hen (about 3 pounds)

3 teaspoons kosher salt

2 tablespoons extra-virgin olive oil

1 guajillo chile, chopped

1 tablespoon achiote paste or annatto powder (available in Latin markets, or in the "international" section of many grocery stores)

1 shallot, minced

3 garlic cloves

¼ cup orange juice

¼ cup freshly squeezed lime juice (from 2 to 3 limes)

1 teaspoon freshly ground black pepper

1 tablespoon ground coriander

1 fresh or frozen banana leaf

12 corn tortillas

2 avocados, peeled, pitted, and sliced

1 cup fresh crema (Mexican sour cream) or sour cream

Pickled Red Onions (recipe follows)

1 cup fresh cilantro leaves

Tastes like chicken. Well, more like pheasant, actually, but guinea hens, or guinea fowl, are a treat if you can find them. If you can't, then you can use chicken. Or a pheasant if you are really ambitious in purveying or hunting.

No matter which bird you use, these tacos are delicious, full of earthy spice and bright with citrus and pickled onions. The technique is inspired by the banana leaf–sheathed whole-pig roasts common in the Yucatán.

1. Preheat the circulator water bath to 71°C / 159.8°F.

2. On a cutting board, lay the hen on its belly and use a pair of kitchen shears to cut away the spine, cutting up toward the neck on either side of the backbone. Cut away the breasts, thighs, and wings. Season the parts well with ½ teaspoon salt and set them aside. Reserve the bones and giblets for another use, such as a stock.

3. In a large cast-iron skillet, heat the olive oil over medium-high heat. When the oil begins to shimmer, add the breasts, thighs, and wings with the skin-side down. Cook until the skin has crisped up a bit, about 4 minutes, and then flip them over. Cook for an additional 4 minutes, or until browned. Remove the skillet from the heat, transfer the hen pieces to a plate, and set it aside.

4. In a blender, combine the guajillo chile, achiote, shallot, garlic, orange juice, lime juice, remaining 2½ teaspoons salt, the black pepper, and coriander. Blend until smooth.

5. On a baking sheet, lay out the banana leaf. Place the breasts, thighs, and wings on the center of the leaf, and pour the sauce from the blender over the meat to coat all the pieces evenly. Fold the banana leaf to make a nice little package.

➤ *Recipe continues*

6. Place the folded banana leaf package in an oven bag, push the air out of the bag as well as you can and seal the bag well with twine. (It's okay if the leaf breaks in the bag, or if some sauce starts to come out of the leaf package inside the bag. The flavor from the leaf will still do its job.) Submerge the bag in the hot water bath for 1 hour; after that, you can hold it there hot until you're ready to finish.

7. Remove the bag from the water bath and let it cool until you are able to handle the hen. While the hen cools, warm up your tortillas one by one for a few seconds in a skillet over medium-high heat, and stack them to retain their warmth. (You can also wrap them in a clean towel to help keep them warm.)

8. Remove the hen from the bag and transfer it to a cutting board. Debone and slice the hen pieces. Arrange the slices on a large platter and surround them with the sliced avocados, crema, corn tortillas, pickled red onions, and cilantro leaves.

9. To build your taco, place some hen slices on a tortilla, top with a slice of avocado, a dollop of crema, some pickled red onions, and a few cilantro leaves. Enjoy!

PICKLED RED ONIONS

Makes 2 cups

I medium red onion, sliced into 1/8-inch-thick rounds

½ teaspoon kosher salt

½ teaspoon sugar

¾ cup distilled white vinegar

2 bay leaves

Place the onions in a container, such as a glass jar, with an airtight lid.

In a medium saucepan, combine 3 cups of water with the salt, sugar, vinegar, and bay leaves. Bring to a boil over high heat, stirring to dissolve the sugar and salt. Remove the pan from the heat and let the brine cool to room temperature.

Once it is cool, pour the brine over the onions in the container and seal it with the lid. Set it aside to pickle for 4 hours.

You can use the pickled onions immediately after 4 hours or store them in the brine, in the fridge, in the same airtight container. They will keep for a week.

CORNISH HENS
Portuguese Style

Prep time: **30 minutes**

Cook time: **1½ hours, plus 20 minutes finishing**

Circulator temperature setting: **72°C / 161.1°F**

SERVES 4

- **2** Cornish game hens (a little under 2 pounds each), giblets removed
- **1 teaspoon** kosher salt
- **6** garlic cloves, minced
- **1 teaspoon** finely grated orange zest
- **2 tablespoons** unsalted butter, at room temperature
- **1 teaspoon** sweet paprika
- **1 tablespoon** extra-virgin olive oil

Sometimes a little chicken is all you need. In this recipe we will spatchcock two Cornish game hens, and then reverse-sear it after cooking it sous vide. To impart a ton of flavor we are going to cook it with six cloves of garlic, a good amount of paprika, and some orange zest. The result is something similar to a Portuguese roasted chicken that I used to get at a neighborhood spot in Montreal years ago. It is tasty on its own but really shines with some rice and beans and a healthy amount of sautéed greens.

1. Preheat the circulator water bath to 72°C / 161.1°F.

2. Arrange the hens on a cutting board with their backs facing up. Using poultry shears or sharp kitchen scissors, run the shears up either side of the backbone. Remove the backbone and reserve it for making some chicken stock at another time. Turn the birds over and open them like a book. Press down firmly on the breasts with the palm of your hand to flatten the birds to a fairly uniform thickness. Season the birds all over with the salt.

3. In a small bowl, combine the garlic, orange zest, butter, and paprika. Slather the flavored butter all over the birds on both sides. Transfer the birds to a resealable gallon-size plastic bag and seal using the displacement method (see page 17). Immerse the bags in the circulator water bath and cook for 1½ hours; after that, you can hold it there hot until you're ready to finish.

4. Remove the hens from the bag and carefully transfer them to a cooling rack. Pat them dry, especially the skin side, with paper towels.

5. Place a large cast-iron pan or two (or work in batches) over medium heat. Add the olive oil, and when the oil shimmers, add the hens skin-side down. (Don't move them around, as that will inhibit the skin from getting nice and

crispy.) Crisp the hens gently until they are golden brown all over, 5 to 10 minutes. Turn the birds over carefully and cook on the second side for a couple minutes, just to get some color. Remove the hens from the skillet and let them rest on a plate for 5 minutes before serving.

TURKEY BREAST TARTINE

with Cranberry Relish, Tarragon,
Butternut Squash, and Frisée

Prep time: **30 minutes**

Cook time: **2½ hours, plus 15 minutes finishing**

Circulator temperature setting: **62°C / 143.6°F**

SERVES 4

1 boneless skin-on turkey breast
   (2 to 3 pounds)

Kosher salt and freshly ground black
   pepper

2 sprigs fresh thyme

1 bay leaf

4 fresh sage leaves

6 tablespoons (¾ stick) cold unsalted
   butter, cubed

2 garlic cloves

3 tablespoons extra-virgin olive oil

1 head frisée, trimmed and
   coarsely torn

¼ cup freshly squeezed lemon juice

2 tablespoons fresh tarragon leaves

4 slices bread (whole-grain, rye,
   or even a baguette), toasted and
   buttered

1 cup Butternut Squash Purée
   (recipe follows)

½ cup Cranberry Relish
   (recipe follows)

I love Thanksgiving food, and once in a while you get a hankering for those flavors but really don't want to invite the entire extended family and Uncle Bob. Turkey is one of those things that, apart from some deli slices in a simple sandwich, most of us eat only once or twice a year. It is just not that common to suddenly up and roast a turkey on a random Tuesday. But now you might. This recipe is kind of a hybrid of a sandwich and those Thanksgiving flavors.

Cooking turkey breast this way is a breeze and results in tender, moist meat every time with no stress—and if you want, no family to deal with.

1. Preheat the circulator water bath to 62°C / 143.6°F.

2. Season the turkey breast with salt and pepper to taste. Place it, along with 1 thyme sprig, the bay leaf, the sage leaves, 4 tablespoons of the butter, the garlic, and a pinch of salt and pepper in a resealable gallon-size plastic bag and seal using the displacement method (see page 17). Submerge the bag in the water bath and cook for 2½ hours; after that, you can hold it there hot until you're ready to finish.

3. Remove the turkey breast from the bag, discarding any liquids. Pat the breast dry with a paper towel.

4. Heat 2 tablespoons of the olive oil in a large skillet set over medium-high heat. When the oil begins to shimmer, add the turkey breast, skin-side down. Cook for 5 minutes or until the skin is golden brown and crispy. Turn the breast over and add the remaining 2 tablespoons butter and the remaining thyme sprig. Cook, basting the turkey breast, for a few minutes more, until the bottom is nicely browned. Remove the skillet from the heat and transfer the turkey

⚞➔ *Recipe continues*

breast to a plate lined with paper towels to soak up the butter. Then thinly slice the turkey breast and set it aside.

5. In a medium bowl, combine the frisée, the remaining 1 tablespoon olive oil, the lemon juice, tarragon, and a pinch of salt. Toss to combine and set aside.

6. To build the tartines, place a slice of toast on each plate. Spread ¼ cup butternut squash purée on each slice, and then add a few slices of turkey breast. Add a spoonful of cranberry relish over the pile of turkey. Top with the frisée salad, then eat!

BUTTERNUT SQUASH PURÉE
Makes about 3 cups

Prep time: **5 minutes**

Cook time: **1½ hours**

Circulator temperature setting: **85°C / 185°F**

2 cups peeled, seeded, and diced butternut squash

1 cup whole milk

1 bay leaf

Kosher salt and freshly ground black pepper

2 tablespoons cold unsalted butter, cubed

Preheat the circulator water bath to 85°C / 185°F.

Combine the squash, milk, bay leaf, a pinch each of salt and pepper, and the butter in a resealable gallon-size plastic bag and submerge it in the hot water bath using the displacement method (see page 17). Cook for 1½ hours.

Remove the bag from the hot water bath and remove the bay leaf. Transfer the remaining contents from the bag to a blender and purée until smooth.

Serve immediately, or store in a sealable container. It will keep in the fridge for up to 5 days.

CRANBERRY RELISH
Makes 2 cups

12 ounces cranberries, fresh or frozen

¾ cup sugar

Freshly grated zest of 2 oranges

1 star anise pod

1 bay leaf

Kosher salt

Combine the cranberries, sugar, orange zest, star anise, bay leaf, and a pinch of salt in a small saucepan and bring to a boil over medium-high heat. Reduce the heat to a simmer and cook for 15 minutes, stirring every few minutes, until the cranberries are completely broken down and a jam-like consistency has been reached.

Remove the pan from the heat and transfer the sauce to a bowl. Let it cool for 20 minutes.

Remove the star anise and bay leaf before serving. The cranberry sauce will keep in a jar in the fridge for about 4 days.

DUCK BREAST

and Warm Mushroom Salad

Prep time: **5 minutes, plus overnight in fridge**

Cook time: **1½ hours for the duck, plus 1 hour for the mushrooms, plus 20 minutes finishing**

Circulator temperature setting: **58°C / 136.4°F for the duck; 85°C / 185°F for the mushrooms**

SERVES 4

4 duck breasts (about 6 ounces each)

Kosher salt

4 sprigs fresh thyme

2 pounds mixed fresh mushrooms, cut into bite-size pieces

1 tablespoon extra-virgin olive oil

1 shallot, finely chopped

1 tablespoon sherry vinegar

1 tablespoon unsalted butter

Pinch of crushed red pepper flakes

1 teaspoon coarsely chopped fresh tarragon leaves

2 tablespoons chopped fresh flat-leaf parsley leaves

¼ cup shaved Parmesan cheese

Duck breast is often mauled by heavy hands. The aim is a crisp skin—with the fat underneath mostly rendered away—and tender flesh with a slight, pleasing gamy flavor, followed by beautiful richness; cooking duck sous vide makes it easy as pie. (Pie is harder.) Speaking of pie, often you see duck paired with fruit, like the ubiquitous duck à l'orange, but here I am aiming toward luxurious earthiness. You can use whatever mushrooms you can find for the warm salad, with shiitakes and oysters providing the closest match to wild mushrooms such as porcini and chanterelles. By all means go with chanterelles and porcini if you have them, or white button mushrooms if that's what you've got. No biggie. Just cook yourself some duck.

1. The day before you plan to cook the duck, score the skin with a sharp paring knife in a diamond grid pattern, making the incisions no more than ⅛ inch deep. (This will allow the fat to render off during the cooking and later searing.) Season the duck breasts all over with about 1 teaspoon salt, cover, and refrigerate overnight.

2. The next day, preheat the circulator water bath to 58°C / 136.4°F.

3. Place the duck breasts and 2 of the thyme sprigs in a resealable gallon-size plastic bag and seal using the displacement method (see page 17). Submerge the bag in the hot water bath and cook for 1½ hours.

4. While the duck is cooking, combine the mushrooms, the remaining 2 thyme sprigs, the olive oil, and a few pinches of salt in a resealable gallon-size plastic bag and seal the same way. Set the bag aside.

⟫→ *Recipe continues*

5. When the duck has finished cooking, remove it from the bag and set it on a plate lined with paper towels. Pat the skin dry to remove any excess liquid and set it aside to rest.

6. Meanwhile, turn the circulator up to 85°C / 185°F. When the circulator reaches that temp, sink the bag of mushrooms into the hot water bath and cook for 1 hour.

7. A few minutes before the mushrooms are done, place a large nonstick or cast-iron skillet over medium heat. Once the pan is hot, add the duck, skin-side down, and sear until skin is brown and crisp, about 5 minutes. Flip and cook for 30 seconds to 1 minute on the other side to lightly brown. Remove the duck from the skillet and transfer it to a plate lined with paper towels to rest.

8. Drain off all but 1 tablespoon of the rendered duck fat from the skillet and raise the heat to medium-high. Add the shallot and cook in the duck fat for 2 minutes. Add the mushrooms and their liquid to the skillet and cook, undisturbed, until the liquid has cooked off and the mushrooms have begun to brown, about 5 minutes. Raise the heat to high and cook for 2 minutes more to crisp the edges.

9. Remove the skillet from the heat and add the sherry vinegar, butter, and red pepper flakes, stirring until the butter has melted. Gently fold in the tarragon, parsley, and shaved Parmesan, and season with salt to taste.

10. Slice the duck against the grain and arrange the slices on individual plates or on a platter. Spoon the warm mushroom salad over the duck and serve.

DUCK CONFIT

with Citrus, Frisée, and
Celery Root Purée

Prep time: **Overnight cure,
20 minutes prep time, plus
optional overnight chilling**

Cook time: **12 hours, plus
20 minutes finishing**

Circulator temperature
setting: **76°C / 168.8°F**

SERVES 4

½ **cup** kosher salt, plus more to taste

1 **tablespoon** light brown sugar

2 **tablespoons** chopped fresh thyme
leaves

½ **teaspoon** yellow mustard seeds

½ **teaspoon** freshly ground black
pepper

½ **teaspoon** fennel seeds

4 duck legs (about 8 ounces each)

1 **cup** duck fat

2 **cups** Celery Root Purée (page 207)

Splash of milk, if necessary

1 navel orange, cut into supremes
(see page 29)

1 ruby red grapefruit, cut into
supremes (see page 29)

1 head frisée, darker leaves discarded

Duck confit is the slow cooking of cured duck legs in duck fat. One of the difficulties with the traditional method in a pot on the stove is finding that perfect simmering temperature—basically you want to poach the legs in the fat so they're tender and moist, not fry them until they're leathery—but with a sous vide setup it is so easy. And since you're cooking the meat surrounded by the fat in a bag, you can do it without having to render enough fat to fully submerge the legs in a big pot, which is the other problem with traditional duck confit: getting or making quarts of duck fat. You can easily render enough fat for this if you are butchering a whole duck, or you can buy just a little duck fat from a butcher or at a better-than-standard grocery store.

The finished dish is crisp duck, succulent under the skin, countered with citrus and frisée, and balanced with some celery root purée. It is a winter delight.

1. The day before you plan to cook the duck, combine the ½ cup salt with the brown sugar, thyme, mustard seeds, pepper, and fennel seeds in a small bowl. Stir well and pour half of this curing mixture into a 10 × 10-inch baking dish. Nestle the duck legs, skin-side up, in the dish. Sprinkle the remaining curing mixture over the duck legs, cover the baking dish with plastic wrap, and refrigerate for 24 hours.

2. The next day, preheat the circulator water bath to 76°C / 168.8°F.

3. Remove the duck legs from the cure and rinse them under cold water. Pat the legs dry with paper towels and place them in a resealable gallon-size plastic bag. Add the duck fat to the bag (don't worry if it is still in solid form, as it will melt when the bag goes in the hot water).

⟫⟶ *Recipe continues*

4. Seal the bag using the displacement method (see page 17), then immerse it into the circulator water bath. Cook for 12 hours; after that, you can hold it there hot until you're ready to finish.

5. Remove the bag from the water bath, pat it dry so you don't make a mess in your fridge, and transfer the bag to the fridge to cool. I like to let the flavors meld and mellow out before using, say 24 hours or so, but it's up to you; you can certainly skip the cooling and finish and serve the duck right away.

6. When you are ready to eat, the finish is really easy. In a small saucepan, warm the celery root purée over medium heat, stirring, and thinning it down with a touch of milk if it needs it (it tends to thicken if it sits in the fridge). Keep it warm over low heat, but stir it frequently to prevent scorching on the bottom.

7. Remove the duck legs from the bag, saving the fat for another use. There will be some fat still clinging to the legs, but that will be what the skin crisps up in, so all good.

8. Place a large skillet over medium heat. Add the duck legs to the skillet, skin-side down, and cook for about 3 minutes, rocking the legs as necessary to get all the skin to contact the pan, until the duck is crispy (and heated through, if you're starting from cold). Flip and sear on the flesh side a minute or two, until browned. Transfer the duck legs to a plate to rest.

9. In a medium bowl, quickly combine the orange and grapefruit supremes with the frisée. Season with a touch of salt. Spoon ½ cup of the celery root purée onto each of four plates and top each with a duck leg. Garnish with the citrus and frisée, and serve.

63.5°C EGGS

Prep time: **1 minute**

Cook time: **1 hour**

Circulator temperature setting: **63.5°C / 146.3°F**

MAKES 6 EGGS

6 large eggs (see Note)

——

Note: This recipe makes 6 eggs, but you can cook up to 36 eggs with a regular circulator if the container is large enough. (If you are cooking 500 eggs, then you can get a kiddie pool and set up 6 circulators. You laugh, but I have done it.)

Built on a simple premise, the 63.5°C egg is one of those rare creations that has reshaped fine-dining culture. Sixty-three-point-five degrees Celsius is the temperature at which the egg yolk is soft and oozing and the white is just barely set around it, like a custard. The 63.5°C egg is luxurious and rich and if you've never experienced it, you'll find that it's a whole new way of appreciating an egg. These days it is the reason why untold numbers of fancy restaurants are adding egg dishes to their menus. Try adding the eggs on top of pasta, or as a "sauce" on pretty much any chicken dish, or in a bowl of hot grits with some crispy roasted vegetables and bacon . . . you will think of a thousand ways to use them before breakfast is over.

The method is a high-tech homage to the Japanese *onsen tamago*—eggs cooked in hot springs (*onsen*). We now have little hot springs in our kitchens, precisely controlled: the circulator bath. The eggs cook for an hour, and then you can turn the temperature down to keep them warm until needed, up to three hours. That's the real trick that chefs love, because three hours is about how long brunch service takes. We ain't dumb, y'all.

1. Preheat the circulator water bath to 63.5°C / 146.3°F.

2. When the water bath comes to temperature, use a slotted spoon to lower the eggs into the water, one by one. No bag needed here—straight-up eggs in a bath. (Be careful not to crack the eggs as you lower them into the water. The eggs sink pretty quickly, and no one likes a busted egg.) Cook for 1 hour. If you want to hold the eggs after that, reduce the temperature of the bath to 55°C / 131°F and hold them hot for up to 3 hours. (Because of a quirk of science, the eggs will actually continue to cook and set even if you lower the temperature, but you have a nice window to work with.)

⇉→ *Recipe continues*

63.5

63

65

67

3. When the eggs are done, remove them from the hot water bath with the slotted spoon. Carefully crack them into a medium bowl. You will see that some of the whites have not set, and that's because the majority of the protein in egg whites is ovalbumin, which sets at 80°C, and thus we will be leaving that behind in liquid form.

4. Fill a smaller bowl halfway with lukewarm water and place it next to the bowl of cracked eggs. Use the slotted spoon again to gently remove the eggs from the medium bowl and dip them in the bowl of water to wash off any remaining ovalbumin. This will give you a cleaner-looking egg. The result will be a smaller egg, but a wonderful one. Use them as you would any poached egg.

5. There you have it—poached eggs, perfect every time.

69

72

BAKED EGGS

in Jars

Prep time: **15 minutes**

Cook time: **1 hour**

Circulator temperature
setting: **70°C / 158°F**

SERVES 4

1 tablespoon unsalted butter

1 medium yellow onion, thinly sliced

Kosher salt

2 cups packed fresh spinach leaves

¼ teaspoon ground nutmeg

2 ounces cave-aged Gruyère cheese, grated

8 large eggs

4 slices whole wheat bread, toasted and buttered

Breakfast in a jar: You open the lid and find a beautiful creamy egg, melted cheese, and greens. You'll need to find some specific (but not hard-to-find) jars: Ball or Kerr brand 8-ounce wide-mouth jars. They are short and squat, and will make for easier eating.

Gruyère is one of those cheeses whose reputations are damaged by mediocre versions, but when you find true cave-aged Gruyère, you will seek it out again and again. It is dotted with a crystalline crunch that results from aging, much like in Parmesan. It is a gem when you find the real thing. Spinach, onions, Gruyère, and eggs with toast. Read the paper while they cook. Simple and good.

1. Preheat the circulator water bath to 70°C / 158°F.

2. In a large skillet over medium heat, melt the butter. When it begins to froth, add the onion and cook, stirring occasionally, for about 10 minutes, until the slices are translucent and have acquired a bit of color. Season with salt.

3. Raise the heat to high and add the spinach and a pinch of salt. Cook for 30 seconds to just wilt the spinach; remove the skillet from the heat. Transfer the spinach and onion to a kitchen towel and wring out the liquid. Transfer the spinach and onion to a bowl. Add the nutmeg and Gruyère and stir to combine. Season with salt.

4. Divide the mixture evenly among four 8-ounce wide-mouth jars. Crack 2 eggs into each jar and sprinkle a pinch of salt over the eggs. Tightly seal the jars with the lids and bands, and then immerse the jars in the circulator water bath. Cook for 1 hour; after that, you can reduce the heat to 55° C / 131°F to hold them hot for up to 3 hours.

5. Remove the jars from the hot water bath and remove the lids. Serve immediately, with toast.

EGG SALAD

Prep time: **20 minutes**

Cook time: **I hour, plus 5 minutes finishing**

Circulator temperature setting: **78°C / I72.4°F**

SERVES 4

8 **large** eggs

2 shallots, minced

1 **cup** minced celery, including the leaves

1 **cup** mayonnaise

¼ **cup** crème fraîche (page 195) or sour cream

1 **tablespoon** freshly squeezed lemon juice

2 **tablespoons** minced fresh dill fronds

1 **teaspoon** Louisiana hot sauce

2 **tablespoons** minced scallions, white parts only

1 **teaspoon** kosher salt

Freshly ground black pepper

I love egg salad, but the consistency of the eggs is my biggest hang-up—it's a bummer when your egg salad is made with rubbery overcooked eggs or with too-soft ones. However, cooking eggs in an immersion circulator produces utter uniformity. Those eggs get in line and follow the rules, and then the celery and shallot come into play and add classic backup to that ovum perfection. Then comes the mayo, the crème fraîche, a touch of dill, a dash of hot sauce, the push of possibility with salt and pepper, all dolloped on toasted bread, resulting in a noontime moment where everything slows and you stare at that sandwich and say, "Damn, that is a great egg salad." (Reminder: When we say eggs, we mean large eggs unless otherwise noted. We also mean the best ones you can buy.)

1. Preheat the circulator water bath to 78°C / 172.4°F.

2. Using a slotted spoon, gently lower the eggs straight into the hot water (being careful not to drop them into the container and crack them) and cook for 1 hour.

3. Five minutes before the eggs have finished cooking, set up an ice bath and place it near the stove. When the eggs are ready, carefully remove them from the water bath and place them in the ice bath to cool.

4. While the eggs are cooling, combine the shallots, celery, mayo, crème fraîche, lemon juice, dill, and hot sauce in a medium bowl and stir to combine.

5. Transfer the cooled eggs from the ice bath to a cutting board. Peel and finely chop the eggs, and add them to the salad base, stirring gently to incorporate. Add the scallions and salt and pepper to taste to the salad and stir again to combine. Serve as a sandwich on your favorite toasted bread.

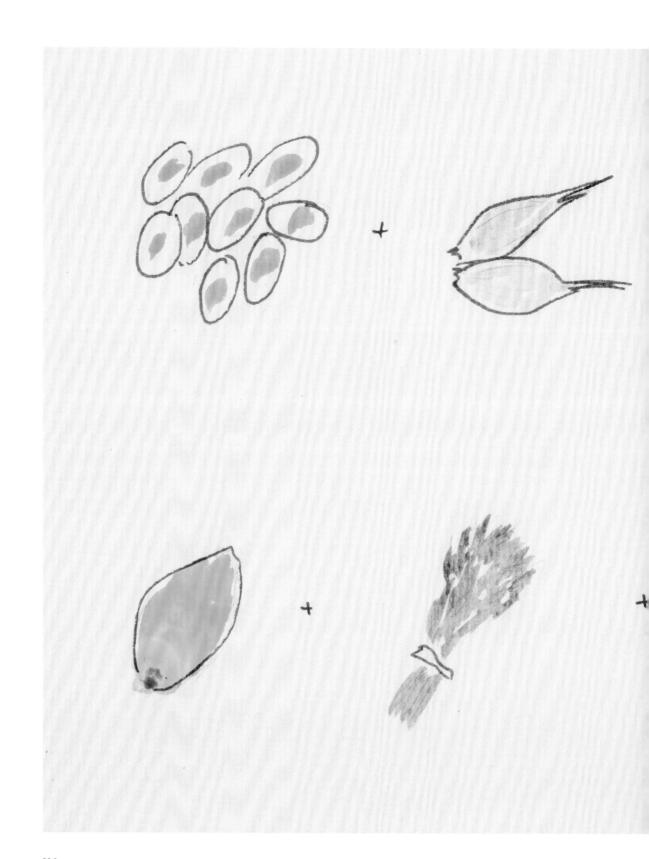

POACHED EGG

Bacon, Cheddar, and Greens Sandwich

Prep time: **As long as it takes you to put everything on the counter**

Cook time: **1 hour**

Circulator temperature setting: **65°C / 149°F**

SERVES 4

4 large fresh eggs

8 slices thick-cut bacon

8 slices good bread

1 large tomato

Kosher salt and freshly ground black pepper

1½ tablespoons unsalted butter, at room temperature

2 tablespoons mayonnaise

4 leaves romaine lettuce

4 slices white cheddar cheese

I have long been a fan of a classic egg sandwich, which really just relies on the simple, timeless, and decadent relationship between an egg and a slice of bacon. Add to this iconic pact a slice of ripe tomato, beautiful lettuce, mayo, and some stunning cheddar and we have a winning way to start your day.

The process is pretty simple on this one, 'cause, duh, it is a sandwich. We will cook the eggs in their shells until the yolks are a light custard and the whites are just setting up; we will cook some thick-cut bacon in a cast-iron pan to make the house smell awesome; we will toast some bread to golden brown; we will slice a tomato and season each slice, diligently, with some salt and pepper; and then we will build a very tasty sandwich that—if the company is great, the coffee is fresh, and the crossword isn't too cryptic—will rival many a fancy Michelin meal. Great meals are what you make them.

1. Preheat the circulator water bath to 65°C / 149°F.

2. Using a slotted spoon, gently place the eggs into the circulator water bath and cook for 1 hour; after that, you can turn the heat down to 55° C /131°F and hold them hot for up to 3 hours.

3. Fifteen minutes before the eggs are ready, cook the bacon in a large skillet over medium heat until it is crisped to your liking. Toast the bread in your toaster or in the broiler. Slice the tomato into thin rounds, and season them with some sea salt and black pepper. Slather 4 pieces of the toast with butter and the other 4 pieces with mayonnaise. Add a piece of lettuce on each mayonnaise side, then the tomato, then the cheese, then the bacon.

4. Remove the eggs from the hot water bath and crack them into a bowl. Use a slotted spoon to remove the eggs from the bowl one at a time, leaving behind any watery whites, and place each one on top of the bacon. Top with the remaining slices of toast.

5. And don't cut those sandwiches! Because the egg is meant to ooze out when you bite into it. Serve with coffee, morning light, and the Sunday crossword.

BEEF & PORK

Beef and pork, like all meat animals, have both prime cuts and working muscles, and historically we recipe writers have worked under a basic assumption: Prime cuts are naturally quite tender and need short cooking times, while working muscles need long, slow cooking to break down and become tender. But beyond those general guidelines, there's a lot of guesswork on time and temperature, which sous vide cooking can help make a thing of the past. From long-cooked Ropa Vieja to perfectly done steaks, this chapter will go through all things bovine and porcine and show how easy the results can be.

That said, great meat cooking starts with great meat. You have many options on how to buy that meat these days, from the old-school butcher in your town who could use your business to online resources that will overnight you the best product in the world at a healthy price. Or you can go my route and just become friendly with the folks in the meat section of your regular grocery store. Ask them to order things for you, ask for advice, have a human-to-human relationship with that person whose job is all things meat. I also shop a lot at Super H Mart, a huge Korean grocery store in the suburbs of Atlanta, one of a nationwide chain. Their selection is massive and they often have cuts that I just don't see elsewhere. Shop around in your neighborhood and you will find the obscure cuts like beef tongue and veal loin, as well as the oft available ones like rib eye and flank.

LONDON BROIL
au Jus

Prep time: **15 minutes**

Cook time: **2 hours, plus 10 minutes finishing**

Circulator temperature setting: **55.6°C / 132°F**

SERVES 4 TO 6

For the London broil

2 garlic cloves, minced

1 teaspoon sweet paprika

½ teaspoon kosher salt

¼ teaspoon freshly ground black pepper

1 teaspoon light brown sugar

1 teaspoon ground coriander

1 teaspoon ground cumin

1 teaspoon chili powder

¼ teaspoon cayenne pepper

2 pounds "London broil" (beef top round steak)

2 tablespoons canola oil

4 to 6 crusty French sandwich rolls

For the jus

1 teaspoon unsalted butter

1 shallot, minced

¼ cup good-quality red wine

1 cup low-sodium beef stock

Kosher salt and freshly ground black pepper

It's confusing, I know. "London broil" is often the name of the cut found on those Styrofoam packs of meat in the supermarket, but technically the term refers to the style of cooking. The muscle, or the butcher's cut, is top round. Anyway, for London broil, marinated meat is cooked and thinly sliced, and then mounded on a warm roll. The beef jus is the lavish dunking sauce on the side. Here we swap in a spice rub for the dry marinade, then cook and reverse-sear. This will ensure that it is not the drab and tough version of London broil that we commonly find, but a tender version packed with flavor.

The jus could be made with a homemade beef stock, but I kind of have a heartfelt connection to canned beef stock. (It's a family thing.) Just buy the reduced-sodium version so it won't stop your heart. The onions and a crusty roll are critical, and you can add a slice of provolone if you want.

Coriander seed is a wonderful thing, but I will insist that you buy it whole and grind it with a mortar and pestle. It is a good workout for the wrist and a surefire way to make sure your ground spices are fresh and redolent.

1. Preheat the circulator water bath to 55.6°C / 132°F.

2. For the London broil, combine the garlic, paprika, salt, black pepper, brown sugar, coriander, cumin, chili powder, and cayenne in a small bowl. Place the meat on a cutting board and rub the spice mixture all over it. Drizzle 1 tablespoon of the canola oil over the meat and make sure it's evenly coated.

➤ *Recipe continues*

3. Transfer the meat to a large resealable plastic bag and seal it using the displacement method (see page 17). Immerse the bag in the circulator water bath and cook for 2 hours; after that, you can hold it hot there until you are ready to finish. In the last hour of cooking, you can make the jus and the onions.

4. On to the "au jus": In a small saucepan, heat the butter over medium heat. When the butter bubbles and froths, add the shallot and cook, stirring, for about 2 minutes, until it has sweated down a bit. Add the red wine and cook for about 5 minutes, until the wine has essentially been reduced to a syrup. Add the beef stock and cook for 5 minutes to marry the flavors. Season with a pinch of salt and some black pepper to taste. Set aside.

5. Remove the bag from the hot water bath and transfer the beef to a cooling rack set over a sheet pan. Heat a large cast-iron pan over high heat and then add the remaining 1 tablespoon canola oil. When the oil is coming to a light smoke, carefully place the beef in the pan and sear it for a total of 4 minutes, rolling the beef every minute or so, until it is nice and golden brown all the way around. Remove the pan from the heat and place the meat on a cutting board. When it is cool enough to handle, shave it thinly against the grain.

6. Mound up the London broil on a crusty sandwich roll and serve with the jus on the side for dunking.

PERFECT STEAKS

with Chimichurri

Prep time: **none**

Cook time: **1 hour, plus 15 minutes finishing**

Circulator temperature setting: **54°C / 129.2°F (for medium-rare)**

SERVES 4

2 New York strips (about 16 ounces each), 1½ inches thick

1½ teaspoons kosher salt

1 tablespoon grapeseed oil

2 tablespoons unsalted butter

2 sprigs fresh thyme

2 garlic cloves

Chimichurri (recipe follows), for serving

Fleur de sel or Maldon sea salt, for finishing

Freshly ground black pepper

This recipe is for New York strip, but it will work for many other cuts, like rib eye, sirloin, tri-tip, tenderloin, and porterhouse. The method is all the same. I am serving this one with a vibrant chimichurri sauce, a mixture of garlic, herbs, oil, and a red wine vinegar that has high acidity to balance the richness of the steak. With any kind of cooking, better ingredients make better food, and with something as simple but luxurious as a steak, get the nicest stuff you can afford. There are plenty of small grass-fed beef farms around the States. Support a good local beef farmer and eat a steak.

This recipe is for a medium-rare steak. I would set it to 49°C / 120.2°F for a rare steak, 56°C / 132.8°F for medium, 61°C / 142°F for medium-well, and crank it up if you like it well done, but then you're on your own.

1. Preheat the circulator water bath to 54°C / 129.2°F.

2. Pat the steaks dry and season them all over with the salt. Place them in a resealable gallon-size plastic bag and seal it using the displacement method (see page 17). Submerge the bag in the circulator water bath and cook for 1 hour; after that, you can hold it there hot until you're ready to finish.

3. Remove the steaks from the bag and place them on a cooling rack set over a sheet pan. Blot them dry with paper towels.

⟫⟶ *Recipe continues*

4. Heat the grapeseed oil in a large cast-iron skillet set over medium-high heat (or high if your stove isn't a fire-breathing dragon). When the oil shimmers, add the steaks to the skillet and sear them for 2 minutes or until nicely browned. Turn the steaks over and add the butter, and when the butter bubbles and froths, toss in the thyme sprigs and garlic cloves. Baste the meat with the butter for 2 minutes, until nicely browned on the second side. Remove the steaks from the skillet, set them on a clean cooling rack, and let them rest for 10 minutes.

5. Carve each steak against the grain. Platter them up and serve with the chimichurri. Season the sliced steak with the finishing salt and freshly ground black pepper as desired.

CHIMICHURRI
Makes about 2 cups

10 garlic cloves, minced

½ cup minced fresh flat-leaf parsley leaves

2 tablespoons fresh oregano leaves

1 tablespoon crushed red pepper flakes, or to taste

¼ cup red wine vinegar

1 cup extra-virgin olive oil

¼ teaspoon kosher salt

Freshly ground black pepper

Combine the garlic, parsley, oregano, and the red pepper flakes in a bowl and stir well. Gradually whisk in the vinegar and olive oil. Season with the salt and with black pepper to taste.

Set the chimichurri aside at room temperature for at least 2 hours to develop its flavor. Keep it in a jar in the refrigerator for up to a week.

PERFECT STEAK, EVERY TIME

Superhero announcer voice: "YOU CAN COOK A PERFECT STEAK EVERY SINGLE TIME WITH THE SUPERCIRCU 3600XE."

It really seems that steak is the reason most people invest in an immersion circulator. You know you like a great steak, you know it's expensive to get the great steak you like, and you know you don't want to screw it up and over- or undercook it. So you get the technology that will make you a precise warden of beef.

Sous vide really does make cooking a great steak a very simple process. But here are a couple more tips to keep in mind: I advise you to season your steak before putting it in the bag, but if you are prepping ahead of time, like days ahead of time, I suggest seasoning it with salt *after* the sous vide process, because as meat sits with salt on it, it is literally curing. I sometimes use a touch of oil in the bag but that is not truly necessary.

Cooking to a specific temperature is the way to make sure you have meat done to your liking—rare, medium-rare, etc. Once the meat hits the temperature you want, it can hang out for a while, even hours, in the sous vide bag without overcooking. But keep in mind that it's not in suspended animation; the meat *will* actually continue to slowly cook and tenderize, like a braise, and get softer even if the temperature is steady. I like my steak to have a bit of chew to it, so I just generally cook it for an hour.

When the temperature has been reached, you have three choices: Remove the steak from the bag, blot it dry with a paper towel, and then immediately sear it in a ripping-hot pan (this is called "reverse searing" because the searing step is usually done at the *beginning* of the cook, not as we're doing here, at the end). Or you can let it hang out in the water bath, holding it at temperature, and then reverse-sear it. Or you can immediately chill the bag in an ice bath and reserve the cooked steak in the fridge until you are ready to reheat by reimmersing it until you hit 40°C / 120°F, sear, and eat it. Remember that if you are serving the steak days after the sous-vide cook, don't salt it until just before searing and serving.

ROPA VIEJA

(Cuban Braised Chuck Roast)
with Plantains

Prep time: **30 minutes**

Cook time: **8 hours, plus
I hour finishing**

Circulator temperature
setting: **58°C / I36.4°F**

SERVES 6 TO 8

1 boneless chuck roast (3 pounds)

1 tablespoon kosher salt

3 tablespoons extra-virgin olive oil

1 large yellow onion, minced

6 whole cloves

2 bay leaves

½ cup beef stock (page 191)

1 cup diced fresh tomato

1 red bell pepper, cored, seeded, and finely diced

6 garlic cloves, minced

1 teaspoon sweet paprika

½ teaspoon ground allspice

½ teaspoon ground cumin

Freshly ground black pepper

Pinch of cayenne pepper

½ cup dry white wine

1 cup chicken stock (page 188)

1 cup diced canned tomatoes

½ cup minced scallions, whites and light green parts only

1 tablespoon red wine vinegar

Stewed Plantains (page 213), for serving

Cooked rice, for serving

Ropa vieja is the national dish of Cuba, a land that means a lot to me because my dear father was born in Havana. The dish is rich braised meat, matched with complex layers of tomato and spices like cloves and cumin and lightened at the end with a splash of good vinegar.

1. Preheat the circulator water bath to 58°C / 136.4°F.

2. Season the chuck roast all over with the salt. Place the roast in a resealable gallon-size plastic bag and add 2 tablespoons of the olive oil, half of the onion, and the cloves, bay leaves, beef stock, and diced fresh tomato. Seal the bag using the displacement method (see page 17) and immerse it in the circulator water bath. Cook for 8 hours.

3. Near the end of the cooking time, prepare an ice bath. When the meat is done, remove the bag from the hot water bath and shock the whole bag in the ice water.

4. When the beef is cool enough to handle, transfer it to a cutting board. Discard the cloves and bay leaves, but save the liquid to use in another recipe. Shred the beef with your hands and set aside. (At this stage, you can refrigerate the meat to finish the dish a day or two later.)

5. In a large pot or Dutch oven over medium-high heat, combine 1 tablespoon olive oil, the remaining onion, the bell pepper, garlic, paprika, allspice, cumin, a couple turns of a pepper mill, and the cayenne. Cook for 10 minutes, stirring often, until the mixture is browning slightly. Deglaze the pot with the white wine and cook it until the sauce is almost dry, about 4 minutes. Add the chicken stock, canned tomatoes, and the shredded chuck roast. Simmer for 30 minutes, stirring frequently.

6. Transfer everything to a serving dish. Finish with scallions and red wine vinegar. Serve with plantains and rice.

CLASSIC CHEESEBURGER

Prep time: **15 minutes**

Cook time: **30 minutes, plus 15 minutes finishing**

Circulator temperature setting: **49°C / 120.2°F**

SERVES 4

2 pounds 80/20 ground beef

1 tablespoon Worcestershire sauce

½ tablespoon kosher salt

1 teaspoon canola oil

4 slices American cheese

4 sesame seed hamburger buns

4 large lettuce leaves (Bibb works great)

4 large tomato slices

4 long dill pickle slices

Condiments (mustard, ketchup, onion slices, your choice)

It might seem like adding work, but cooking burgers with the sous vide method will make your grill days much faster and easier, and ultimately more consistently delicious. The key is understanding the temperature you want to achieve. I like my burger medium-rare, so I am aiming for a temperature of 49°C / 120.2°F. This is lower than a steak temperature for a similar degree of doneness, but because the burger is thin, the searing will quickly bring it up above that.

The other great thing about the sous vide method for a burger is that you can fully chill the bags in an ice bath after the immersion cooking, and then store them in the fridge for 4 to 5 days. This means the start-to-finish time on your burger dinner can be about 10 minutes on those days.

And just in case you didn't know what 80/20 means in the ingredients list, it is the lean-to-fat ratio in ground meat. You commonly find 70/30, 80/20, 85/15, or 90/10 in the grocery store. The more fat, the richer and moister the burger; the more lean, the deeper the meat flavor. The really lean blends will make a fine burger but tend to be on the drier side of the spectrum, so cooking them sous vide to get the temperature just right is especially helpful.

1. Preheat the circulator water bath to 49°C / 120.2°F.

2. In a large bowl, combine the beef, Worcestershire sauce, and half of the salt, and stir lightly until just fully incorporated. Transfer the mixture to a resealable gallon-size bag. Place the bag on the counter, and using a rolling pin, gently roll the beef to an even thickness in the bag, making sure the beef goes to all corners of the bag, pushing the air out. Seal the bag. The result will be a ¾-inch-thick, gallon-size patty of ground beef. Yep.

⫸→ *Recipe continues*

3. Next, without piercing the bag, take a very dull straightedge (like the top of a ruler or the back of a butter knife) and press it into the outside of the bag—in the middle from north to south, and then again in the middle from east to west—to equally divide the large patty into 4 squares. (YES, THEY WILL BE SQUARE, like those of a chain fast-food burger place that rhymes with "*Vendy's.*") Submerge the bag in the circulator water bath and cook for 30 minutes; after that, you can hold it there hot until you're ready to finish.

4. A few minutes before the burgers are finished cooking, set a cooling rack over a sheet pan.

5. Remove the bag from the hot water bath and carefully transfer the burgers to the rack. Use a paper towel to pat the burgers dry on both sides and let them rest for 10 minutes.

6. Set a large cast-iron skillet (or a grill) over high heat. Brush the canola oil over both sides of the burgers. When the skillet is screaming hot, add the burgers to the skillet and sear them until a nice crust forms, a minute or so, then flip and repeat. Remove the burgers from the skillet and top each one with cheese while the patties are still hot.

7. It's time to build those burgers. If you like your bun toasted, toast it. I like lettuce, tomato, pickle, onion, ketchup, and mustard on my burgers, but you can do whatever floats your boat. Hell, add mayo if you want!

KOREAN SHORT RIBS

with Shiitake Mushrooms, Wilted Bok Choy,
and Toasted Peanuts

Prep time: **30 minutes, plus
12 to 24 hours in fridge**

Cook time: **16 hours,
plus 10 minutes finishing**

Circulator temperature
setting: **70°C / 158°F**

SERVES 4

½ **cup** soy sauce

½ **cup** light brown sugar

¼ **cup** honey

¼ **cup** Asian sesame oil

2 **tablespoons** mirin (sweet rice
wine for cooking)

5 garlic cloves: 4 left whole,
1 thinly sliced

4 scallions

1 Asian pear, peeled, cored, and
coarsely diced

3 **pounds** short ribs, kosher cut

½ **cup** raw peanuts

2 **tablespoons** extra-virgin olive oil

½ shallot, minced

1 **pound** fresh shiitake mushrooms,
stems removed, sliced into ½-inch
pieces

6 small heads bok choy, trimmed, cut
into 1½-inch pieces

2 **tablespoons** fish sauce

1 **tablespoon** rice vinegar

1 **tablespoon** freshly squeezed
lime juice

Often Korean short ribs are very thin slices of bone-in short rib, used for fast-cooking Korean barbecue, but this is more of a classic braise using Korean-ish flavors. Sesame, peanuts, fish and soy sauces, all meld together in this recipe and get finished with mushrooms and bok choy. It is a beauty of a dish.

"Kosher cut," when it comes to ribs, means the cut is made across the rib bones, as opposed to with them, as is the case for "English cut" short ribs. "Flanken" is a thicker slice of kosher cut style ribs, and that is what we want here. Because of the tougher nature of the ribs, these need to cook for a very long time, so you can either drop them into the bath the night before or wake up really early and eat late. You can, as always, arrest the cooking process by fully chilling the bag in an ice bath once the sous vide time is finished, and then pick up the final steps later on.

1. In a food processor or a blender, combine the soy sauce, brown sugar, honey, sesame oil, mirin, whole garlic cloves, scallions, and the Asian pear. Blend the marinade until smooth.

2. Add the short ribs to a resealable gallon-size plastic bag and pour the marinade into the bag. Seal the bag and refrigerate it for at least 12 hours, or up to 24 hours if you want.

3. Preheat the circulator water bath to 70°C / 158°F.

4. Remove the ribs from the bag and discard the marinade. Return the ribs to the bag and seal it using the displacement method (see page 17). Submerge it in the circulator water bath and cook for 16 hours. (Keep an eye on the level of water in the bath, adding more water if necessary.)

➤ *Recipe continues*

5. Ten minutes before the ribs are finished cooking, place a medium skillet over medium heat. Add the peanuts and toast them, shaking the pan so they don't burn, until they are well colored and fragrant, about 5 minutes. Remove the skillet from the heat and transfer the peanuts to a plate to cool. Once they are cool enough to handle, coarsely chop the peanuts and set them aside.

6. Turn on the broiler to high. Set a wire rack on a sheet pan.

7. Remove the bag from the hot water bath, and when it is cool enough to handle, transfer the ribs to the wire rack, discarding any liquids left in the bag. Broil the ribs for 10 minutes, flipping them halfway through, until a nice crust forms.

8. While the short ribs are broiling, prepare the shiitake mushrooms and bok choy: Heat the olive oil in a large skillet over medium-high heat. When the oil begins to shimmer, add the shallot and the sliced garlic and cook until they are tender, about 2 minutes. Add the mushrooms and cook until they have released a decent amount of liquid, about 2 minutes. Add the bok choy and cook for another 2 minutes, until wilted.

9. Remove the skillet from the heat and stir in the fish sauce, rice vinegar, and lime juice. Transfer the shiitakes and bok choy to a platter and top with the crisped short ribs that you've just removed from the broiler. Garnish with the toasted peanuts. Eat!

SEARED TRI-TIP

with Salsa Verde

Prep time: **15 minutes**

Cook time: **2 hours, plus 20 minutes finishing**

Circulator temperature setting: **58°C / 136.4°F**

SERVES 4

1 tri-tip steak (about 2 pounds)

Kosher salt and freshly ground black pepper

2 sprigs fresh thyme

1 garlic clove, smashed

2 cups coarsely chopped fresh tomatillos

1 cup coarsely chopped sweet yellow onion

1 cup packed fresh cilantro leaves and stems

2 tablespoons freshly squeezed lime juice

1 teaspoon ground cumin

1½ tablespoons sliced seeded serrano chiles

2 tablespoons extra-virgin olive oil

Tri-tip is a triangular steak cut from the bottom sirloin, with a little more rigor and bite than tenderloin, but tasting remarkably similar. The trick is to slice it against the grain, which changes a fair bit as you carve it. Pay attention and make sure you are cutting against it—across the muscle fibers, not alongside them.

This recipe is total summer to me. If you want to finish it on a hot grill instead of the cast-iron pan, go at it.

1. Preheat the circulator water bath to 58°C / 136.4°F.

2. Season the tri-tip with salt and pepper to taste and place it in a resealable gallon-size plastic bag. Add the thyme sprigs and garlic and seal the bag using the displacement method (see page 17). Submerge the bag in the circulator water bath and cook for 2 hours; after that, you can hold it there hot until you're ready to finish.

3. Ten minutes before you're ready to take the tri-tip out, make the salsa verde: In a blender, combine the tomatillos, onion, cilantro, lime juice, cumin, and serranos. While blending on low speed, slowly drizzle in 1 tablespoon of the olive oil. Continue to blend until the sauce is smooth. Season with salt to taste and set aside.

4. Remove the bag from the hot water bath and transfer the steak to a plate lined with paper towels. Pat the steak dry, blotting off any excess moisture, and discard any remaining thyme or garlic.

5. In a large skillet over high heat, heat the remaining 1 tablespoon olive oil. When the oil starts to shimmer, add the steak to the skillet and sear it for 2 minutes on each side, or until a nice crust forms. Remove from the pan and let it rest on a cutting board for 8 minutes. Slice the tri-tip against the grain and serve it with the salsa verde.

CORNED BEEF

Prep time: **5 minutes, plus 1 week brining, plus 20 minutes**

Cook time: **48 hours**

Circulator temperature setting: **57°C / 136.4°F**

SERVES 6

- 2 **cups** apple juice
- 2 **tablespoons** maple syrup
- 1 **teaspoon** Instacure #1 (optional; see Note)
- 1 **teaspoon** yellow mustard seeds
- ½ **teaspoon** whole black peppercorns (I like Tellicherry peppercorns here)
- 1 **teaspoon** caraway seeds
- ½ **teaspoon** allspice berries
- 4 bay leaves
- ½ **cup** kosher salt
- 1 **quart** ice cubes
- 4 **pounds** beef brisket (fatty or lean, up to you)
- 1 **tablespoon** extra-virgin olive oil
- 1 medium sweet yellow onion, halved
- 1 **cup** beef stock (page 191)
- 2 **tablespoons** brown miso paste
- 4 garlic cloves
- 1 **tablespoon** unsalted butter

Note: Instacure #1, also called Prague Powder #1, curing salt, or pink salt, is a staple of butcher shops and charcuterie kitchens. It prevents harmful bacteria from making your cured meats nasty, and it gives the product that characteristic pink ham color. Find it online or at a butcher shop.

When you are growing up in Ottawa or Montreal, corned beef becomes an important part of your life. Brisket in a panoply of preparations is very popular up there above the border. This version is both classic and easy, but is also contemporized with the umami-rich addition of miso. It takes a fair bit of time—a weeklong brine and a gentle two-day cook. Prepare in advance, and plan a couple of meals. It is worth it.

1. In a large saucepan, combine 1½ quarts cold water with the apple juice and bring to a boil. Add the maple syrup, Instacure if using, mustard seeds, peppercorns, caraway seeds, allspice berries, bay leaves, and salt. Cook for 3 minutes at a rapid boil, then remove from the heat. Add the ice cubes and set aside; wait for the brine to come to room temperature.

2. Place the brisket in a large nonreactive container, then pour the brine over the brisket until it is completely covered. Cover with a lid or plastic wrap and refrigerate it for 1 week.

3. After 1 week, remove the brisket, and strain the brine, discarding the liquid and keeping the spices. Set aside the beef and the strained spices.

4. Preheat the circulator water bath to 57°C / 136.4°F.

5. In a large skillet, heat the olive oil over medium-high heat. Add the onions to the skillet and cook, turning them every once in a while, until they are well browned and a touch charred, about 15 minutes.

➤ *Recipe continues*

6. Place the brisket, charred onions, beef stock, miso paste, garlic, butter, and the reserved strained spices in a large oven bag. Sink the bag into the circulator water bath using the displacement method (see page 17), then tie off the oven bag with twine. Cook the brisket for 48 hours. (Make sure you monitor the water level in the circulator bath, adding more as needed; a lid or covering the water bath with plastic wrap is a really good idea.)

7. If you are going to serve the brisket right away, remove it from the bag as soon as it is cool enough to handle. Then slice and serve or use it for hash. Or, if you are going to serve it later, make an ice bath. Cool the brisket, still in the bag, in the ice bath for 30 minutes, then pat it dry, and store it in the fridge for up to 2 weeks. To reheat, rewarm it gently in a large pot with a cup of water. Cover the pot and gently simmer until warm throughout, about 30 minutes. Slice the brisket across the grain or plate it up at brunch in a Crisped Corned Beef Hash with Eggs (recipe follows).

CRISPED CORNED BEEF HASH WITH EGGS
Serves 4

Prep time: **5 minutes if you're working with cooked ingredients**
Cook time: **20 minutes**

6 tablespoons (¾ stick) unsalted butter
I large sweet yellow onion, diced
I serrano chile, stemmed, seeded, and thinly sliced
½ pound cooked corned beef, chopped
2 pounds cooked new potatoes, diced
4 large eggs
Kosher salt and freshly ground black pepper
Hot sauce, for serving

Place 4 tablespoons of the butter in a large nonstick or cast-iron skillet set over medium-high heat. When the butter begins to bubble and froth, add the onion and cook until it begins to soften, about 4 minutes. Add the serrano chile, corned beef, and potatoes. Using a spatula, combine the ingredients in the skillet and then gently press them into an even layer. Raise the heat to high and cook, undisturbed, until the bottom is golden brown, 3 minutes.

Stir the hash again and once more press the ingredients into an even layer. Cook for 3 minutes. Repeat this process one more time, until the potatoes and brisket are well browned. Reduce the heat to low and cook for 5 minutes.

In a separate large cast-iron or nonstick skillet, melt the remaining 2 tablespoons butter over medium-high heat. Crack the eggs into the skillet and cook to your desired doneness.

To serve, place a large heap of crispy corned beef hash on each plate. Top each heap of hash with a fried egg. Season with salt and pepper to taste, and serve it with some hot sauce on the side and a good cup of coffee. Eat it up.

FLANK STEAK

Stuffed with Spinach, Ricotta, and Red Bell Peppers

Prep time: **30 minutes**

Cook time: **6 hours, plus 20 minutes finishing**

Circulator temperature setting: **57°C / 134.6°F**

SERVES 4

2 cups fresh spinach leaves

1 cup fresh ricotta cheese

½ cup chopped roasted red bell peppers (see Note, page 80)

2 garlic cloves, minced

1 tablespoon freshly grated lemon zest

Kosher salt and freshly ground black pepper

1 flank steak (about 2 pounds)

2 tablespoons extra-virgin olive oil

Flank steak is a well-marbled cut from the belly of the cow. It is an excellent cut of meat, full of flavor but easily overcooked and made tough. Not here, though. This recipe calls for the steak to be butterflied and then stuffed in a classic Italian style. Don't get scared with the rolling and trussing part. It is easy once you give it a whirl. It goes great with some Herby New Potatoes (page 246).

1. Preheat the circulator water bath to 57°C / 134.6°F.

2. Bring a saucepan of salted water to a boil over high heat. Quickly blanch the spinach, then shock it in cold water. Squeeze it dry, and chop it.

3. In a medium bowl, combine the spinach, ricotta, roasted bell peppers, garlic, and lemon zest and mix well. Season with salt and pepper to taste, and set side.

4. On a cutting board, lay the flank steak out flat and cover it with plastic wrap. Using a meat tenderizer, a mallet, or a small heavy saucepan, gently pound the flank steak to flatten until it is ⅛ inch thick. Remove the plastic wrap and spread the spinach-ricotta mixture evenly over one side of the flattened steak. Using your best burrito rolling skills, carefully roll the steak over the spinach-ricotta mixture, constantly pulling it toward you to keep it as tight as possible. Using butcher's twine, truss the stuffed flank steak every 1½ inches to keep it from unrolling.

5. On a flat surface next to the trussed steak, lay down another large piece of plastic wrap. Place the trussed steak on one end of the plastic wrap and tightly wrap the steak in the plastic wrap to make a firm roll (in fancy French kitchen talk, this is a *torchon*, named for the side towel that would have been used to torque the meat). Tie off both ends of the

⫸ *Recipe continues*

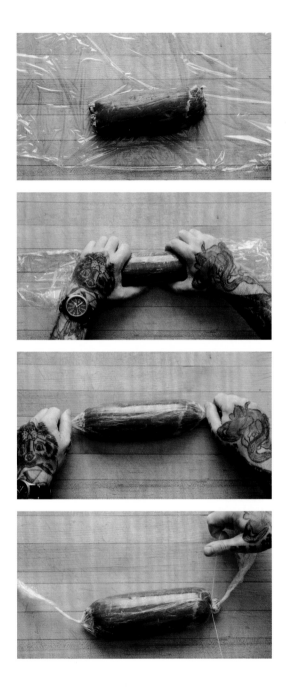

torchon with butcher's twine. Place the torchon in a resealable gallon-size plastic bag and seal the bag using the displacement method (see page 17). Submerge it in the circulator water bath. Cook for 6 hours; from there, you can hold it hot until you're ready to finish the dish.

6. Remove the bag from the hot water bath. Pull the torchon from the bag and let it rest for 5 minutes.

7. Remove the plastic wrapping from the flank steak and pat the meat dry with paper towels. Heat the olive oil in a large skillet over medium-high heat. When the oil is shimmering, add the flank steak and sear until you see some good coloring on each side, about 2 minutes per side. Transfer the steak to a cooling rack or a plate lined with paper towels and let it rest for 10 minutes.

8. Remove the twine, slice the stuffed flank steak into 1- to 1½-inch pieces, and serve.

PORK RIBS

with Guajillo BBQ Sauce

Prep time: **20 minutes, plus overnight in the fridge**

Cook time: **12 hours, plus 10 minutes finishing**

Circulator temperature setting: **74°C / 165.2°F**

SERVES 4

2 **tablespoons** ground cumin

2 **tablespoons** ground coriander

¼ **teaspoon** ground white pepper

1 **tablespoon** ground guajillo chile

1 **tablespoon** light brown sugar

1 **tablespoon** kosher salt, plus more to taste

5 **pounds** pork ribs

2 **tablespoons** extra-virgin olive oil

½ sweet yellow onion, minced

4 garlic cloves, chopped

8 guajillo chiles, stemmed and seeded

1 **(14-ounce)** can diced tomatoes

1 **cup** honey

1½ **cups** cider vinegar

Ribs like long cook times and precise temperatures. This is a long way from a backyard smoker, a method I love, but with a sous vide setup I can get some sleep without fanatically checking the temperature and stoking the fire during the night.

The sauce is a new classic for your repertoire—sweet and tart as you'd expect a barbecue sauce to be, but with the bite and fruity-smoky flavor of guajillo chiles. Guajillo chiles are fairly readily available in the Hispanic section of a super store or at your local Mexican grocery. I have five Mexican groceries, all phenomenal, within a mile of me in Athens, Georgia. Embrace your inner chile aisle.

1. In a medium bowl, combine the cumin, coriander, white pepper, ground guajillo chile, brown sugar, and 1 tablespoon salt and stir until everything is incorporated. This will be your spice rub.

2. On a cutting board, cut the pork ribs into 4 racks. Liberally season the ribs with the spice rub and let them sit, covered, in the refrigerator overnight.

3. The next day, preheat the circulator water bath to 74°C / 165.2°F.

4. Remove the ribs from the refrigerator, transfer them to a resealable gallon-size plastic bag, and seal it using the displacement method (see page 17). Sink the bag into the circulator water bath and cook for 12 hours; after that, you can hold them there hot until you're ready to finish. Be sure to replace the water in the bath as necessary.

⟫→ *Recipe continues*

5. Forty-five minutes before the ribs are ready to be removed from the water bath, make the guajillo barbecue sauce: Heat the olive oil in a medium saucepan over medium-high heat. When the oil begins to shimmer, add the onion and cook for 4 to 5 minutes, until it is starting to brown in spots. Add the garlic and cook for 2 minutes, until golden brown and fragrant. Add the chiles, tomatoes, and 2 cups of water and bring the mixture to a boil. Reduce the heat to a simmer and cook for 25 minutes, uncovered, stirring often. Remove from the heat and let cool for about 10 minutes.

6. Transfer the tomato mixture to a blender and blend until it has the consistency of a paste. Add the honey and vinegar, and purée until a nice smooth consistency is achieved. If the sauce seems too thick, thin it out with a little more water, or if it's too loose, gently simmer it a bit to reduce it. Season the sauce with salt to taste and set it aside.

7. Set the broiler on your oven to high. Set a wire rack on a sheet pan.

8. Remove the ribs from the bag and discard any liquids. Place the ribs on the wire rack, pat them dry with paper towels, and broil for 3 to 4 minutes, until a nice crust forms.

9. Remove the ribs from the broiler and spoon a few tablespoons of the guajillo barbecue sauce over them. Place the ribs back under the broiler for 2 to 3 minutes more, until the sauce begins to bubble and brown a bit. Remove the ribs from the oven, transfer them to a platter, and serve with extra guajillo barbecue sauce on the side. Eat 'em up, and don't forget the napkins.

PORCHETTA
on Ciabatta

Prep time: **30 minutes**

Cook time: **24 hours, plus 15 minutes finishing**

Circulator temperature setting: **68°C / 154.4°F**

SERVES 6 TO 8

½ **cup** chopped fresh flat-leaf parsley leaves

½ **cup** chopped fennel fronds

6 garlic cloves, minced

1 **tablespoon** freshly grated orange zest

1 **tablespoon** fennel seeds, toasted

1 **tablespoon** coriander seeds

1 **teaspoon** crushed red pepper flakes

1 **tablespoon** kosher salt

1 **(3-pound)** slab skin-on pork belly, about 10 × 6 inches

Freshly ground black pepper

1 pork tenderloin, silver skin removed (about 1 pound)

½ **cup** extra-virgin olive oil

6 to 8 ciabatta rolls

2 **cups** fresh arugula leaves

Aioli (recipe follows)

True porchetta is a whole young pig, deboned, rubbed with herbs and fennel seed, stuffed with the liver, and then trussed up tightly and cooked on a spit. It is an ambitious meal to make at home. This version is much more within the realm of possibility. It is a skin-on pork belly, butterflied, rubbed with a heady mix of herbs and spices, inlaid with a pork tenderloin, and cooked sous vide. It is then crisped up and served. It is lovely on bread with arugula and aioli, so I have followed with an aioli recipe.

1. Preheat the circulator water bath to 68°C / 154.4°F.

2. In a medium bowl, combine the parsley, fennel fronds, garlic, orange zest, fennel seeds, coriander seeds, red pepper flakes, and ½ tablespoon of the salt; stir until everything is evenly distributed. This is your herb mixture. Set it aside.

3. Place the pork belly on a cutting board, skin-side down, with the wider side of the belly parallel with the bottom edge of the cutting board. With a sharp knife, butterfly the belly by starting your incision halfway through the thickness at the edge closest to you. Cut, uniformly, up to the top, as though you were opening a book, leaving the top uncut (this is the "spine" of the book). Flop the pork open. Rub the herb mixture evenly into the exposed meat of the belly. Season generously with pepper and the remaining ½ tablespoon salt.

4. Place the pork tenderloin near the top of the butterflied belly, parallel with the edge of the cutting board. Rotate your cutting board 180 degrees. (This will make it so the skin ends up on the outside as you roll it up.) Tightly roll the belly around the tenderloin, and then truss it tightly with butcher's twine. (I use 6 to 8 loops for a porchetta that's 10 inches wide, which is what you should have in front of you.) Take a very sharp paring knife and prick about

≫→ *Recipe continues*

30 pricks through the skin of the belly, but not much deeper; try not to poke it into the meat beneath. This will allow the fat to render as the pork cooks. Wrap the pork tightly in plastic wrap, place it in a large resealable plastic bag, and seal it using the displacement method (see page 17). Immerse the bag in the circulator water bath and cook for 24 hours; after that, you can hold it there hot until you're ready to finish. Make sure to replenish the water in the circulator bath when needed. (Covering the bath with a lid or plastic wrap is a great idea.)

5. Remove the bag from the hot water bath and unwrap the porchetta from both the bag and the plastic wrap, leaving the twine intact. Pat it with a paper towel until it is dry to the touch.

6. Heat the olive oil in a large skillet over medium-high heat. Carefully add the porchetta and cook, using tongs to turn it every 2 minutes or so, until it is crispy, about 10 minutes. (You can also baste it with the hot fat for more browning.) Let it rest for 10 minutes.

7. Carve the porchetta into round slices. I find a bread knife is your friend in this carving, to get through the crisp pork skin cleanly. Serve it on ciabatta rolls with arugula and aioli to your taste.

AIOLI
Makes 1 cup

1 large egg yolk, organic, local, and all that
1 small garlic clove, finely minced
¼ teaspoon kosher salt
¼ cup grapeseed oil
¼ cup good-quality extra-virgin olive oil
Pinch of cayenne pepper
1 tablespoon freshly squeezed lemon juice
Freshly ground black pepper

In a medium bowl, whisk together the egg yolk, 2 teaspoons of room-temperature water, and the garlic. Add the salt, and then slowly whisk in the grapeseed oil in a thin stream, pouring it from a measuring cup. Add the olive oil in the same way. You will now have a mayonnaise. Season it with the cayenne, lemon juice, and black pepper to taste. Whisk it up and transfer it to a jar until ready to use. It will keep in the fridge for a week.

PÂTÉ DE CAMPAGNE

Prep time: **1 hour**

Cook time: **2½ hours, plus 1 hour cooling**

Circulator temperature setting: **65°C / 149°F**

2 **pounds** lean pork butt, coarsely ground

5 **ounces** pork fatback, diced

5 **ounces** chicken livers, cleaned of any veins or discolored spots, puréed or minced

4 garlic cloves, minced

½ medium sweet yellow onion, puréed

2 large eggs, whisked well

½ **cup** heavy cream

½ **cup** cognac

2 **teaspoons** kosher salt

1 **tablespoon** crushed red pepper flakes

½ **teaspoon** ground mace

½ **teaspoon** ground nutmeg

½ **teaspoon** ground cloves

½ **teaspoon** freshly ground black pepper

½ **teaspoon** Instacure #1 (optional; see Note, page 137)

½ **cup** roasted pistachios, coarsely chopped

1 **tablespoon** freshly grated lemon zest

1 **pound** sliced smoked bacon

Bread, mustard, and pickles, for serving

This is a classic pâté, a rustic beauty that's meaty with pork and pork fat, deep with chicken liver, and mellowed out with cognac and cream. Terrines, or pâtés, are a delight to make, and cooking them sous vide is definitely the way to go. Because we know that moisture is retained and meat is completely cooked at 65°C / 149°F, we can hold that temperature and ensure a consistent result. This is the type of food that I want you to develop confidence in. It will open so many doors to the culinary world, and soon you will dream of opening up a place called Mes Terrines in the South of France. Not a bad dream to have. Use a terrine mold if you have one, or otherwise a loaf pan would work just fine. (Terrine molds are small, deep, heavy rectangular baking dishes with a vented lid. Le Creuset makes some beautiful ones of enameled cast iron.) Get your bread, mustard, and pickles ready for an adventure.

1. Preheat the circulator water bath to 65°C/ 149°F.

2. In a large bowl, combine the ground pork butt, pork fatback, chicken livers, garlic, and onion. Mix well and set aside in the fridge, as you finish the rest of the prep.

3. In another large bowl, whisk the eggs, cream, and cognac together until the eggs are well beaten. Add the salt, red pepper flakes, mace, nutmeg, cloves, black pepper, and Instacure (if using) and whisk until well incorporated.

4. Remove the meat mixture from the fridge, and using a large spoon, stir the egg mixture into the meat until it is completely incorporated. Add the pistachios and lemon zest and mix until everything is well combined and resembles the texture of uncooked meatloaf. This mixture is called a farce. Cook a small bite of the farce in a hot skillet as you would breakfast sausage, taste it, and adjust the seasoning

>→ *Recipe continues*

if needed. (You can even do it in a microwave; the idea is just to taste it for seasoning and not to have to eat a bite of raw pork.)

5. Line a terrine mold or a loaf pan with plastic wrap, letting any excess hang over the edges. Line the mold with the bacon slices, arranging them across the width of the mold and making sure to overlap them so they will enclose the farce (let the ends hang over the sides). Pack the mold to the top with the farce, pressing down to remove any air pockets. Fold the loose bacon ends over the farce and then wrap any excess plastic wrap over the bacon. Tightly wrap the terrine mold, without its lid, with plastic wrap, making sure to wrap it from end to end, then from side to side.

6. Place the terrine mold in a large resealable plastic bag and seal it using the displacement method (see page 17). Sink the bag into the circulator water bath and cook for 2½ hours.

7. Shortly before the terrine is done cooking, prepare an ice bath.

8. Remove the bag containing the terrine from the hot water bath and transfer the bag to the ice bath. Let it cool for 1 hour.

9. Remove the bag from the ice bath and remove the terrine mold by slowly lifting up on the plastic wrap. Carefully unwrap the terrine mold and place it upside-down on a cutting board. Lift the mold off the pâté and remove the rest of the plastic wrap. Slice and serve the pâté with bread, mustard, and pickles. The pâté will keep in the fridge for a week, well wrapped in plastic wrap.

DOUBLE-CUT PORK CHOP

with Roasted Apples and Vidalias

Prep time: **15 minutes, plus 24 hours brining**

Cook times: **3 hours for onions (includes 30 minutes for apples), plus 1½ hours for pork and 15 minutes finishing**

Circulator temperature settings: **80°C / 176°F for the onions and apple, and then 56°C / 132.8°F for the pork chops**

SERVES 4

3 tablespoons kosher salt

1 tablespoon light brown sugar

2 sprigs fresh thyme

6 bay leaves

2 double-cut pork chops (1 pound each)

1 large Vidalia onion

2 tablespoons unsalted butter

1 teaspoon coriander seeds

1 tablespoon red wine vinegar

2 red apples (use a variety that keeps its shape during cooking, such as Gala)

2 tablespoons honey

1 cup dry white wine

1 cup chicken stock (page 188)

2 tablespoons extra-virgin olive oil

12 fresh sage leaves

A double-cut pork chop is a bone-in pork chop with two rib bones still attached. It is twice the thickness of a regular pork chop. This makes complete sense.

In this recipe, the brined chops get seared and then served alongside some super-soft slow-cooked sweet onions and apples. This also makes complete sense.

1. The day before your pork chop dinner, make a brine by bringing a quart of water to a boil in a saucepan, adding the salt, brown sugar, thyme sprigs, and 4 of the bay leaves. Cook, stirring occasionally, until the salt and sugar have dissolved in the boiling water. Turn off the heat and cool the brine to at least room temperature.

2. Grab the pork chops and place them on a cutting board. If they are laden with silver skin and sinew, get a sharp paring knife and scrape them to remove that silver skin. Place the pork chops in an airtight container and cover them with the brine until the meat is submerged. Cover and refrigerate for 24 hours to chill out.

3. The day of your pork chop dinner, preheat your circulator water bath to 80°C / 176°F.

4. Cut the onion in half lengthwise, from top to bottom. Peel off the skin and trim the root end (but do not trim too much, as we want the root end to keep the onion layers together during cooking). Place the onion halves in a large, resealable plastic bag and add 1 tablespoon of the butter, the coriander seeds, and the vinegar. Seal the bag using the displacement method (see page 17), submerge it in the circulator water bath, and cook for 3 hours.

▶▶▶ *Recipe continues*

5. Thirty minutes before the onions are done, core the apples, and with the skin still on, cut them into half-inch-thick rounds. Place the apples in a resealable gallon-size plastic bag, add the honey and the white wine, seal as above, and add the bag to the hot water bath; cook for 30 minutes.

6. Five minutes before the apples are finished cooking, prepare a large ice bath. When they are done, remove the bag of apples and shock the bag in the ice water. Remove the onions as well and shock the bag in the same ice water. Set aside.

7. Reduce the temperature of your circulator water bath to 56°C / 132.8°F.

8. Remove the pork chops from the brine and pat them dry. Discard the brine. Place the chops in a resealable gallon-size plastic bag and add the chicken stock, remaining 2 bay leaves, and remaining 1 tablespoon butter. Seal as above, submerge in the hot water bath, and cook for 1 hour; after that, you can hold them there hot until you're ready to finish.

9. Remove the pork chops from the circulator bath, transfer them to a cooling rack, and let them rest for a moment.

10. Heat the olive oil in a large cast-iron skillet over medium-high heat. Pat the pork chops dry with paper towels and add them to the skillet. Sear until they are nicely browned, about 2 minutes on each side. Transfer the chops to a cutting board (reserve the skillet with its oil and drippings) and let them rest for 3 minutes while you cook the onions, apples, and sage.

11. Drain the onions and the apples, discarding their liquids. In the reserved cast-iron skillet, cook the sous vide onions and apples over medium-high heat for 2 minutes per side to get some color on them. Add the sage leaves and cook for 1 minute more, until the leaves are crispy.

12. Carve the chops thinly against the grain, as you would a bone-in rib eye. Place the pork on a platter and serve with the onions, apples, and sage. Eat!

PORK LOIN

with Coriander, Orange, Ground
Guajillo, and a Cucumber Salad

Prep time: **30 minutes**

Cook time: **2 hours, plus 20 minutes finishing**

Circulator temperature setting: **62°C / 143.6°F**

SERVES 6

- **1 tablespoon** ground coriander
- **1 tablespoon** ground guajillo chile
- **2 tablespoons** freshly grated orange zest
- **1 teaspoon** kosher salt, plus more to taste
- **1 boneless pork loin** (3 pounds)
- ½ **cup** freshly squeezed orange juice
- **3 tablespoons** extra-virgin olive oil
- ½ English cucumber, sliced into ¼-inch-thick rounds
- **2 tablespoons** freshly squeezed lime juice
- **2 tablespoons** fresh cilantro leaves
- **2 tablespoons** fresh mint leaves, torn

Pork with orange and chiles, punched up with the floral brilliance of coriander seed, makes me think of Cuban food. My father was born in Havana and lived there until the revolution, when he moved to Canada. (They were Canucks to begin with, but my grandfather was a banker in the Caribbean.) After forty years away from Cuba, my dad started teaching for a month each year at the University of Havana. Life comes full circle. This recipe is for you, Pops.

1. Preheat the circulator bath to 62°C / 143.6°F.

2. In a medium bowl, combine the coriander, guajillo chile, orange zest, and 1 teaspoon salt. Set aside.

3. On a cutting board, remove any silver skin and trim any excess fat from the pork loin. Liberally coat the pork with the spice mixture and transfer it to a resealable gallon-size plastic bag. Add the orange juice and seal the bag using the displacement method (see page 17). Submerge the bag into the circulator water bath. Cook for 2 hours; after that, you can hold it there hot until you're ready to finish.

4. Remove the pork loin from the bag, place it on a paper-towel-lined plate, and pat it dry. Heat 2 tablespoons of the olive oil in a large skillet over medium-high heat. When the oil begins to shimmer, add the pork loin. Sear for 9 minutes total, 3 minutes per side (let's pretend it has three sides), until the loin is nicely browned. Transfer the pork loin to a cooling rack to rest for 10 minutes.

5. While the pork loin rests, combine the cucumber and lime juice in a medium bowl. Season with a pinch of salt and toss to coat the cucumber well. Add 1 tablespoon olive oil, the cilantro, and the mint, and season with additional salt to taste. Toss again. Slice the pork loin and serve it with the fresh cucumber salad alongside.

PORK BELLY

with Herb Citrus Salad

Prep time: **30 minutes**

Cook time: **12 hours, plus 30 minutes to chill, plus 20 minutes finishing**

Circulator temperature setting: **77°C | 170.6°F**

SERVES 4

- 1 **(2-pound)** slab pork belly, skin off
- 1 **tablespoon** kosher salt
- ¼ **cup** chicken stock (page 188)
- 1 **sprig** fresh thyme
- 1 bay leaf
- 2 garlic cloves
- 1 **tablespoon** soy sauce
- 1 **tablespoon** fish sauce (optional)
- 1 **tablespoon** canola or grapeseed oil (or any other high-heat neutral oil)
- 2 **tablespoons** Chinese black vinegar
- ½ English cucumber, thinly sliced lengthwise and then cut into 2-inch-long planks
- ¼ **cup** diagonally sliced scallions
- ¼ **cup** fresh parsley leaves
- 2 seedless clementines, washed well and sliced into wedges

Bacon is pork belly but not all pork belly is bacon. This is a luscious dish in which rich seared pork belly is generously balanced by the acidity of crunchy cucumber, sweet clementines, and the flavors of fish sauce, Chinese vinegar, and soy sauce.

Make sure you get skin-off pork belly. It is much easier to work with in this type of recipe.

1. Preheat the circulator water bath to 77°C / 170.6°F.

2. Season the pork belly all over with the salt. Combine the pork belly, chicken stock, thyme sprig, bay leaf, garlic cloves, soy sauce, and fish sauce (if using) in a resealable gallon-size plastic bag and seal it using the displacement method (see page 17). Submerge the bag in the circulator water bath and cook for 12 hours; after that, you can hold it there hot until you are ready to finish. Be sure to check the water level every few hours, making sure it is above the bag.

3. Remove the bag from the hot water bath, place it between two sheet pans or large plates, and place something heavy (like extra plates) on top to weight it down and compress the pork belly. This compression will help achieve a uniform texture and cooking surface when you sear the pork. Place this arrangement in the refrigerator and leave it until the pork is fully chilled, about 30 minutes.

4. Take the pork out of the bag, reserving the liquid in a bowl. Place the pork belly on a plate lined with paper towels to absorb any excess moisture. Transfer the pork to a cutting board and cut it into 4 equal pieces.

➤ *Recipe continues*

5. Heat the oil in a large skillet set over medium-high heat. When the oil starts to shimmer, add the pork belly pieces, fat-side down. Gently and carefully press down on the belly with a metal spatula to make sure there is good contact between the belly and the pan. Pan-roast the pork belly, turning the pieces often to get some good color on all six sides, about 10 minutes total. Transfer the pork to a plate lined with paper towels and let it rest for 5 minutes.

6. While the pork is resting, warm 1 cup of the reserved sous vide liquid in a small pot. Add the vinegar and keep the mixture warm at a bare simmer. In a small bowl, toss the cucumber, scallions, parsley leaves, and clementine slices together. Dress the salad with the vinegared liquid to taste.

7. Place the pork belly pieces on a platter and arrange the salad artfully over the pork. Drizzle with a bit more of the vinaigrette and serve.

BEEF TONGUE

with Gribiche

Prep time: **10 minutes**

Cook time: **36 hours, plus 10 minutes finishing**

Circulator temperature setting: **77°C / 170.6°F**

SERVES 6 AS AN APPETIZER

1 beef tongue (2 to 3 pounds)

½ yellow onion, sliced

2 Roma tomatoes, quartered

2 tablespoons kosher salt

¼ cup pork fat or duck fat

3 sprigs fresh thyme

3 garlic cloves

2 tablespoons Gribiche (recipe follows)

I grew up eating tongue, so I am cool with it. People who say "*ewww*" about tongue have no idea how awesome it is; it has an incredibly beefy flavor that is rich and almost buttery. Because it is a working muscle beyond compare, it does like a long cook time in liquid, and so this is not the sort of thing to jiffy up for a quick snack. But it *is* the kind of thing a very long, gentle, consistent sous vide cook time is perfect for. This dish works great as an appetizer. You can also make a pretty stellar sandwich if you're into that sort of thing. I just happen to love sandwiches.

Gribiche will keep in the fridge for a week, and it is one amazing condiment to have around. It takes poached salmon or even a simple roast chicken to a new level. Make too much and use it up over the week.

1. Preheat the circulator water bath to 77°C / 170.6°F.

2. In a resealable gallon-size plastic bag, combine the tongue, onion, tomatoes, salt, pork fat, thyme, and garlic. Seal the bag using the displacement method (see page 17) and cook for 36 hours. (Keep an eye on the water level. You may need to add more over the course of the cook time.)

3. Fifteen minutes before the tongue is ready, prepare an ice bath.

4. When the tongue has finished cooking, remove the bag from the hot water bath and plunge it into the ice bath to cool for 15 minutes.

Recipe continues

5. Remove the bag from the ice bath and transfer the cooled tongue to a cutting board. Discard the bag and the liquids.

6. Using a paring knife or a vegetable peeler, carefully remove the tough outer skin from the tongue. Thinly slice the tongue and arrange the slices in a single layer on a platter or large plate. Garnish with a spoonful of gribiche and serve.

GRIBICHE
Makes about 1 cup

1 hard-boiled egg, minced

1 shallot, finely minced

3 teaspoons capers, minced

3 teaspoons cornichons, minced

2 teaspoons Dijon mustard

2 tablespoons sherry vinegar

½ cup extra-virgin olive oil

1 teaspoon fresh tarragon leaves, minced

1 teaspoon fresh parsley leaves, minced

1 teaspoon minced fresh chives

Kosher salt

In a medium bowl, combine the egg, shallot, capers, cornichons, mustard, vinegar, olive oil, tarragon, parsley, and chives and stir until well incorporated. Season with salt to taste. Serve, or cover and store in the fridge. It will keep for 1 week.

VITELLO TONNATO

Prep time: **1 hour**

Cook time: **1 hour, plus 40 minutes cooling and finishing**

Circulator temperature setting: **48°C / 118.4°F**

SERVES 4 TO 6 AS AN APPETIZER

For the veal

1 pound trimmed boneless veal loin

1 teaspoon kosher salt

1 cup chicken stock (page 188)

1 sprig fresh flat-leaf parsley

2 bay leaves

2 sprigs fresh thyme

1 celery stalk, cut into 4-inch lengths

1 large carrot, halved lengthwise and cut into 3-inch lengths

1 medium yellow onion, halved

For the sauce

¼ cup good-quality canned tuna

2 tablespoons chicken stock (page 188)

1 teaspoon rinsed and chopped canned anchovies

1 tablespoon capers

1 tablespoon whole-grain mustard

½ cup extra-virgin olive oil

2 tablespoons freshly squeezed lemon juice

Kosher salt and freshly ground black pepper

To finish

1 cup finely sliced mustard greens

¼ cup celery leaves

¼ cup thin sliced carrot rounds

¼ cup celery brunoise (from 1 to 2 stalks)

¼ cup pitted sliced Kalamata olives

Classics mean a lot to me. It means they have been tested by chefs and cooks and pros and amateurs. It means they are well-worn roads that have stood the test of time and brought us to a better eating place. *Vitello tonnato* is one of those dishes: thin-sliced veal with a rich sauce made by emulsifying tuna and olive oil. When I order it in a restaurant that has integrity, I am pretty sure I am going to be happy.

I know that veal loin is not likely to be in the regular arsenal in your fridge, but I implore you to find some sustainably and humanely raised veal (it does exist) and get cracking. This is an appetizer portion, but you can always double up the recipe if you want to have it as a main, with an old Dolcetto or a cold Peroni . . . you be you.

Oh, and lest you are thrown by the word *brunoise*, it is a term for meticulous tiny dice.

1. Cook the veal: Preheat the circulator water bath to 48°C / 118.4°F for rare (see page 120 if you prefer a different doneness). Tie the veal with kitchen twine to hold its shape during cooking. Season the veal all over with the salt and place it in a resealable gallon-size plastic bag. Add the chicken stock, parsley, bay leaves, thyme sprigs, celery, carrot, and onion and seal the bag using the displacement method (see page 17). Immerse the bag in the circulator water bath and cook for 1 hour; after that, you can hold it there hot until you're ready to finish.

2. Five minutes before the veal has finished cooking, prepare an ice bath. When the veal is done, plunge the bag into the ice bath and let it cool there for 30 minutes. Then transfer the bag to the fridge until ready to serve.

➤ *Recipe continues*

3. When you are ready to serve the veal, make the sauce: Drain the tuna, put it in a blender, and add the chicken stock, anchovies, capers, and mustard. Purée until smooth. Then, with the motor still running, slowly drizzle in the olive oil and purée until emulsified. Add the lemon juice, season with salt and pepper to taste, and blend well to combine.

4. To finish: Slice the cold veal very thin and arrange the slices evenly on individual plates. Liberally drizzle the veal with the tonnato sauce, and then garnish it beautifully with the mustard greens, celery leaves, carrot coins, celery brunoise, and olives. Eat.

LAMB (& A RABBIT STEW)

The great food writer Waverly Root wrote that "the United States is sulky towards lamb." He was not wrong, but I think that is changing. If you pick up a cookbook from twenty years ago, there will likely be references to lamb from the U.S. being "gamey" when compared to Australian or New Zealand lamb. Our farms have come a long way since then, and I think American lamb is some of the best lamb in the world.

In this chapter we will explore some of the classic lamb dishes that work well in a sous vide scenario. From lamb rack in a classic British fashion to leg in a purist Italian style to shanks that hug the cuisines of North Africa, I will show you the perfect results you can get with proper temperatures and a slow roll.

The final recipe in the chapter is for rabbit, a recipe with Burgundian overtones of mustard, thyme, and mushrooms. Rabbit is another meat that is gaining traction, and it has always had a small but ardent following in North America. It's tasty, like a sophisticated cousin to chicken, and it can be very environmentally friendly to produce. We should eat a lot more of it. The historic problem with rabbit cookery is that it is a very lean meat and can be easily overdone. Sous vide takes that issue and shelves it, with precision.

BONELESS LEG OF LAMB

with Classic Italian Salsa Verde

Prep time: **30 minutes**

Cook time: **2 hours, plus 20 minutes finishing**

Circulator temperature setting: **57°C / 134.6°F**

SERVES 6

1 boneless leg of lamb (4 pounds)

Kosher salt and freshly ground black pepper

2 tablespoons extra-virgin olive oil

Salsa Verde (recipe follows)

This is a beautiful spread of perfectly rosy slices of lamb with a punchy, rustic parsley-lemon-caper sauce. You can often find a boneless-rolled-and-tied leg of lamb in your average grocery store. Lamb is a grass-fed meat that is more environmentally sound to produce than beef, and it's just delicious.

1. Preheat the circulator water bath to 57°C / 134.6°F

2. First, we are going to butterfly the leg of lamb. Let's take this step by step. Boneless lamb leg is usually sold in an elastic string net. Remove that and place the lamb on a cutting board so that the smoother side (where the outer haunch would have been facing out) is facedown. Use a sharp paring knife to carefully cut into the leg to remove any excess fat, hard gristly bits, and silver skin. (If you don't know what silver skin is, you'll know it when you see it.) Start from the center of the meat and work outwards, working around the muscles, and leave that outer haunch area intact. Don't worry about totally cleaning out all the sinew and so on. The braising time will take care of the rest. We are working from the middle and moving outwards, slowly flattening the leg to a uniform thickness. It will now look like a rather misshapen butterfly. Season it all over with salt and pepper. Roll the leg tightly (like a burrito) and truss it with butcher's twine every inch or so to keep it from unrolling. (I have managed to do this with embroidery thread, knitting yarn, and some vines on occasion. I am MacGyver at heart.)

3. Now, let's torque. Roll the whole trussed leg in plastic wrap and twist one end tight, tying it off tightly with twine. The other end can then be tightened well by twisting the plastic wrap in the opposite direction and then tying it off with more twine.

⋙ *Recipe continues*

4. Place the trussed and torqued lamb in a large oven bag and seal it using the displacement method (see page 17), tying the end off tightly with twine. Submerge the bag in the circulator water bath and cook for 2 hours; after that, you can hold it there hot until you're ready to finish.

5. Remove the bag from the hot water bath, remove the lamb from the bag, remove the plastic wrap from the lamb, and place the lamb on a cooling rack or a plate lined with a paper towel. Pat the lamb dry with paper towels to remove any excess moisture.

6. Heat the olive oil in a large skillet over medium-high heat. When the oil begins to shimmer, add the lamb and sear it for 10 minutes, about 5 minutes per side, until the outside begins to brown and crisp. Transfer the lamb to a clean cooling rack and let it rest for 10 minutes.

7. To serve, thinly slice the lamb and arrange the slices on a platter. Spoon a nice helping of salsa verde over the lamb. Eat.

SALSA VERDE
Makes about 2 cups

1½ cups chopped fresh flat-leaf parsley leaves

2 tablespoons capers, chopped

4 canned anchovies, chopped

2 garlic cloves, minced

1 tablespoon freshly grated lemon zest

1 tablespoon white wine vinegar

1 tablespoon freshly squeezed lemon juice

⅔ cup extra-virgin olive oil

Kosher salt and freshly ground black pepper

In a medium bowl, combine the parsley, capers, anchovies, garlic, and lemon zest. Slowly drizzle in the vinegar and lemon juice, using a fork to blend. Gadually add the olive oil and season the salsa with salt and pepper to taste. Continue to blend with a fork until it is smooth. You can store the salsa in a tightly covered jar in the fridge for up to a week.

LAMB SHANKS

with Currants, Cinnamon, and Dates

Prep time: **35 minutes**

Cook time: **10 hours, plus 30 minutes finishing**

Circulator temperature setting: **60°C / 140°F**

SERVES 4

2 **tablespoons** canola oil

1 medium yellow onion, coarsely chopped

2 celery stalks, coarsely chopped

2 large carrots, coarsely chopped

4 Roma tomatoes, chopped

1 **teaspoon** cumin seeds

2 cinnamon sticks (3 inches each)

1 **teaspoon** coriander seeds

1 red jalapeño pepper, minced

4 American lamb hind shanks

1 **teaspoon** kosher salt

Freshly ground black pepper

2 **cups** chicken stock (page 188)

½ **cup** dried currants

16 medjool dates, pitted

½ **cup** torn fresh mint leaves

Harissa, for serving

Cooked couscous, for serving

Picture a lamb. It can be in a pasture, eating grass and just being lamb-y. Look at its legs. The shank is the part of the leg just above the ankle that goes to the mid-shin. Look at the difference between the forelegs and the hind legs: The forelegs are skinnier, while the hinds are meaty and muscular. I want you to find lamb hind shanks from a butcher whose name you know or from a farmer you have a relationship with.

In this recipe, those shanks will be succulent, infused with the flavors of North Africa, inspired by the fine writing of Paula Wolfert. Paula had a huge influence on me in my younger days of cooking. I soaked up her books, especially *Couscous and Other Good Food from Morocco* and *The Cooking of the Eastern Mediterranean.*

Currants are bush berries. Though they look like raisins, currants are tart and more savory than their dried grape counterpart. If you can't find them, however, you can use raisins in a pinch.

1. Preheat the circulator water bath to 60°C / 140°F.

2. In a large saucepan, warm the canola oil over medium heat. Add the onion and cook until translucent, about 5 minutes. Add the celery, carrots, tomatoes, cumin seeds, cinnamon sticks, coriander seeds, and jalapeño, and cook until the celery and carrots are starting to soften, 5 minutes. Remove the pan from the heat.

⟫→ *Recipe continues*

3. Place the lamb shanks on a sheet pan and season them with the salt and with black pepper to taste. Place the shanks in a large oven bag and add the cooked vegetable mixture and the chicken stock. Submerge the bag in the circulator water bath. Using the displacement method (see page 17), tie off the top of the oven bag with twine. Cook for 10 hours; after that, you can hold it there hot until you are ready to finish.

4. Twenty minutes before the lamb is done, preheat the oven to 375°F.

5. When the lamb is done, carefully remove the bag from the hot water bath and transfer the shanks to a large baking dish. Strain the braising liquid into the baking dish (discard the solids), and scatter the currants and dates over the shanks. Roast on the middle rack of the oven for 30 minutes. The top will develop a little color and texture, the liquid will tighten up a bit, and it will smell delicious.

6. To serve, garnish the lamb shanks with the torn mint, and serve it with some spicy harissa and steamed couscous.

LAMB LOIN

with Fava Beans, Cherry Tomatoes,
and Garlic Vinaigrette

Prep time: **10 minutes**

Cook time: **3 hours, plus 20 minutes finishing**

Circulator temperature setting: **57°C / 134.6°F**

S E R V E S 4

1 boneless lamb loin (2 pounds), silver skin and excess fat removed

Kosher salt and freshly ground black pepper

2 sprigs fresh thyme

1 sprig fresh rosemary

2 cups peeled fresh fava beans

2 tablespoons extra-virgin olive oil

1 cup cherry tomatoes, halved

2 tablespoons fresh parsley leaves

2 tablespoons torn fresh mint leaves

3 tablespoons Garlic Vinaigrette (recipe follows)

Lamb loin is a beautiful treat and rivals the rack, in my opinion, as the most prized cut. It is also the easiest cut of lamb to cook perfectly, with its uniform thickness and shape. As the gastronome Hannibal Lecter noted, lamb and favas have a spring affinity, and tomatoes and garlic just add more to that relationship. Just don't be as creepy as Hannibal.

1. Preheat the circulator water bath to 57°C / 134.6°F.

2. Liberally season the lamb loin with salt and pepper. Place the lamb in a resealable gallon-size plastic bag, add the thyme and rosemary sprigs, and seal the bag using the displacement method (see page 17). Submerge the bag in the circulator water bath and cook for 3 hours; after that, you can hold it there hot until you're ready to finish.

3. Bring a quart of water to a vigorous boil in a small pot. While the water is heating, prepare a small ice bath.

4. Add a teaspoon of salt to the boiling water, and then add the favas. Cook for 1 minute and then use a slotted spoon to scoop them out and submerge them in the ice bath to chill and stop the cooking. Then drain the cooled favas.

5. Remove the bag from the hot water bath and transfer the lamb loin to a plate lined with a paper towel. Pat it dry with paper towels.

6. Heat the olive oil in a large skillet over medium-high heat. When the oil begins to shimmer, add the lamb and sear it for 6 minutes, 3 minutes per side, until it is well browned. Remove the lamb from the skillet and let it rest for 10 minutes on a wire rack or on a plate lined with a paper towel.

➠➔ *Recipe continues*

7. While the lamb rests, make the fava bean and tomato salad: In a medium bowl, combine the favas, tomatoes, 1 tablespoon of the parsley, and 1 tablespoon of the mint. Add the garlic vinaigrette and toss. Season with salt and pepper to taste.

8. To serve, slice the lamb loin into ¼-inch-thick rounds. Arrange them on a large plate and spoon the dressed favas and tomatoes on top. Garnish with the remaining 1 tablespoon each of parsley and mint.

GARLIC VINAIGRETTE

Makes 1 cup

3 garlic cloves, minced

Freshly grated zest of 1 lemon

⅓ cup freshly squeezed lemon juice (from 2 lemons)

1 cup extra-virgin olive oil

1 teaspoon Dijon mustard

Kosher salt and freshly ground black pepper

In a pint-size mason jar, combine the garlic, lemon zest, lemon juice, olive oil, mustard, and a pinch of salt and pepper, and shake vigorously until well blended. Season with additional salt and pepper to taste. The dressing will keep in the refrigerator for about a week. (Be sure to give it a nice shake every time you use it, because it will separate.)

LAMB RACK
with Mint Sauce

Prep time: **15 minutes**

Cook time: **1 hour, plus 20 minutes finishing**

Circulator temperature setting: **52°C / 125.6°F**

SERVES 4

- 2 **tablespoons** minced fresh rosemary leaves
- 2 **tablespoons** minced fresh flat-leaf parsley leaves
- 3 garlic cloves, minced
- 1 **teaspoon** crushed red pepper flakes
- 1 lamb rack, chine bone removed, Frenched (about 2 pounds prepped)
- 1 **teaspoon** kosher salt
- Freshly ground black pepper
- ¼ **cup** extra-virgin olive oil
- 1 **teaspoon** fine sea salt
- ¼ **cup** red wine vinegar
- ½ **cup** finely minced fresh mint leaves
- 1 **teaspoon** sugar
- 1 **tablespoon** canola oil

This recipe is a classic in the English style, finished with a decidedly British mint sauce. The temperature noted here will cook the lamb to a perfect medium-rare so it is warmed through and rosy, not the chewy red that you often see. Also, lamb racks usually have seven or eight bones on them. Try to find one with eight bones so one person doesn't feel left out of the two-bone party.

1. Preheat the circulator water bath to 52°C / 125.6°F.

2. Combine the rosemary, parsley, garlic, and red pepper flakes in a small bowl and stir until blended.

3. Season the lamb rack liberally with the kosher salt and with black pepper, and press the herb-garlic mixture into the meat on all sides. Place the herbed rack in a resealable gallon-size plastic bag and seal it using the displacement method (see page 17). (Work a little carefully because we do not want the bones to pierce the bag.) Submerge the bag in the circulator water bath and cook for 1 hour; after that, you can hold it there hot until you're ready to finish.

4. While the lamb is cooking, combine the olive oil, sea salt, vinegar, mint, and sugar in a small bowl. Whisk well and set the mint sauce aside.

5. Remove the bag from the hot water bath and transfer the lamb to a cooling rack. Pat the lamb with a paper towel to dab away the excess moisture and let it rest for 5 minutes while you heat up a large cast-iron skillet over medium-high heat.

6. When the skillet is hot, add the canola oil and sear the lamb for 3 minutes per side, until nicely browned. Transfer it to a cutting board and let it rest for 5 minutes. Then carve the lamb and serve it on a platter with the mint sauce.

RABBIT STEW

with Mustard, Thyme, Watercress,
and Shaved Button Mushrooms

Prep time: **30 minutes**

Cook time: **3 hours**

Circulator temperature
setting: **60°C / 140°F**

SERVES 4

- **1** cleaned rabbit (2 to 3 pounds)
- **1 teaspoon** kosher salt
- **½ cup** all-purpose flour
- **2 tablespoons** canola oil
- **2** shallots, minced
- **1** large carrot, sliced diagonally
- **1** celery stalk, minced
- **2 tablespoons** whole-grain mustard
- **1 tablespoon** chopped fresh thyme
  leaves
- **2 cups** chicken stock (page 188)
- **½ cup** crème fraîche (page 195)
- **1 cup** fresh watercress sprigs
- **6** button mushrooms
- Sea salt

When cooked well, rabbit is delicious, meaty with a hint of game flavor, and remarkably environmentally friendly to raise. But rabbit is often overcooked and has never broken into the mainstream culinary world because it is a finicky lean protein. Cooking it is a matter of precision or it becomes dry and makes you revert to the ubiquitous chicken. Sous vide fixes this by accurately cooking it to a temperature that shows off the beauty of rabbit with tender and tasty results.

Rabbit butchery is much like chicken, oddly enough. In this recipe, we will butcher down the rabbit, remove the hind legs and forelegs, and get the rib cage out, but leave the backbone in. This is a classic braise with flavors that have always been cozy with rabbit: mustard, thyme, watercress, carrot, and mushrooms. Let's get cooking.

1. Preheat the circulator water bath to 60°C / 140°F.

2. Place the rabbit with its back down on a cutting board. With a sharp knife, remove each hind leg at the hip joint by pulling the leg away from the body and angling the joint up to show you where to cut it to create a smooth separation. (If you've done this with a chicken, it's almost the same thing.) Take kitchen shears and cut out the breastbone by cutting up along either side of it, freeing up access to the rib cage. Carefully run a knife under the ribs and cut them away. Remove the forelegs with the knife and set aside. Cut the main body into four saddle cuts with the backbone still in place. Season the hind legs, forelegs, and saddle pieces evenly with the salt and then dredge them in the flour, shaking off any excess.

3. Heat the canola oil in a large cast-iron skillet over medium-high heat until it is shimmering. Add the floured rabbit pieces and sear until they are golden brown, about 2 minutes. Turn the rabbit pieces over and sear for 2 minutes on the other side.

4. Transfer the rabbit pieces to a sheet pan and keep the skillet on the heat. Add the shallots, carrot, and celery to the skillet and cook, stirring once in a while, to soften, about 2 minutes. Add the mustard, thyme, chicken stock, and crème fraîche, and cook for 2 minutes more.

5. Place the rabbit pieces, along with the vegetables and liquid from the skillet, in a resealable gallon-size plastic bag and seal it using the displacement method (see page 17). Submerge the bag into the circulator water bath and cook for 3 hours; after that, you can hold it there hot until you're ready to serve.

6. Carefully transfer the rabbit, vegetables, and the juices to a large serving dish and garnish with the watercress. Use a mandoline to thinly shave the mushrooms over the dish. Season with sea salt as desired.

STOCKS, SAUCES, ETC.

Stocks are the basis of great food in so many ways.
Professionally, if I couldn't lean on the goodness of bright,
luscious, golden chicken stock, I would feel a little lost. But
there are so many stocks to make up the backbone of your
cooking, and so many sauces and condiments to provide that
finishing touch. This chapter will show you the virtues of
creating flavor-packed stocks, sauces, and condiments using
the sous vide setup. It may seem odd to cook a liquid inside
another liquid, but this method produces clean, clear results,
pure flavor, and won't reduce away if you forget about it for a
while. And there are a few cool sauces and items here that are
just super easy to make with sous vide—like yogurt and tomato
sauce. From ham stock to crème fraîche, this chapter will show
you a better way to stock your kitchen with the foundations of
great food.

VEGETABLE STOCK

Prep time: **15 minutes**

Cook time: **6 hours**

Circulator temperature setting: **85°C / 185°F**

MAKES 2 TO 3 QUARTS

- **3 cups** sweet yellow onions, cut into a large dice
- **2 cups** carrots, cut into a large dice
- **2 cups** celery, cut into a large dice
- **2** garlic cloves, halved
- **4** bay leaves
- **2 sprigs** fresh thyme
- **1 tablespoon** whole black peppercorns
- **1 tablespoon** coriander seeds

_____

Note: Because we are submerging 2-quart jars into the water bath, you'll need a pretty deep water bath.

With 2-quart mason jars, you can make some beautiful stocks. The process is easy and the result is a productive add to your larder. I cook the stock, strain it, and portion it out into smaller containers that freeze well. In a pinch, wide-mouth glass jars make great freezing containers, as long as you leave some space at the top for expansion of the stock as it freezes. Do not use regular-mouth jars because the curve in the jar can break upon freezing.

The malaise of vegetable stocks is the waft of overcooked vegetables, but sous vide solves that with a precise temperature, below a boil, producing a stock with clarity and foundational flavor to be used in whatever application you like. Most vegetable stocks are boiled and extract a lot of flavors that taste astringent and have the attractive odor of a compost pile. This will keep your vegetable stock sweet and consistent.

1. Preheat the circulator water bath to 85°C / 185°F.

2. Evenly divide the onions, carrots, celery, garlic, bay leaves, thyme sprigs, peppercorns, and coriander seeds between two 2-quart mason jars, or divide them among smaller jars. Fill the jars with cold water to 1 inch below the top and then cap each jar with the lid and band, tightening the bands to finger-tight. Submerge the jars in the circulator water bath and cook for 6 hours, occasionally adding water if necessary to keep the jars submerged. (Or cover the bath with plastic wrap.)

3. Using a jar lifter or a pair of tongs, a towel, and some dexterity, remove the jars from the hot water bath. Strain the stock into a large container and discard the solids. Let the stock cool to room temperature.

4. Thoroughly wash the mason jars, pour the cooled vegetable stock back into them, and store in the fridge. Use within 4 days or freeze for up to 6 months.

ROASTED CHICKEN STOCK

Prep time: **10 minutes**

Cook time:**30 minutes roasting, then 5 hours**

Circulator temperature setting: **85°C / 185°F**

MAKES 2 QUARTS

2 pounds chicken bones and giblets (no livers)

1 tablespoon extra-virgin olive oil

1 cup red wine

1 medium yellow onion, quartered

2 celery stalks, cut into 1-inch pieces

2 medium carrots, cut into 1-inch pieces

1 tomato, coarsely chopped

2 sprigs fresh thyme

4 whole black peppercorns

½ teaspoon coriander seeds

2 bay leaves

Chicken stock is the foundation a lot of my professional cooking rests on. When it's great, chicken stock is an elixir that only helps make food taste great. To me it tastes like a calming restorative, a role it has taken on in many cultures, redolent with thyme, subtle hints of onion and celery, mellowed out with the soulful richness of schmaltz. Use the gizzard and heart, neck and feet, if they were included with your bird, but never use the liver. Store those in the freezer until you have enough to make a mousse.

As with all stocks, this will freeze well. Just be sure to use straight-sided glass jars, not the curved small-mouth ones, which have a tendency to break when expansion happens in the freezer.

1. Preheat the oven to 425°F and preheat the circulator water bath to 85°C / 185°F.

2. Using a cleaver, cut the chicken bones into pieces that are small enough to fit into 1-quart mason jars.

3. In a large mixing bowl, combine the bones, giblets, and olive oil. Toss well and then lay the bones and giblets out in one layer on a rimmed baking sheet. Place the baking sheet in the oven and roast for 30 minutes.

4. Remove the baking sheet from the oven and pour away the chicken fat. (Or you can save it for another use if you want.) Reserve the baking sheet.

5. Divide the bones and giblets evenly between two 1-quart mason jars. Place the baking sheet on the stove so that it covers two burners and pour the wine into the baking sheet. Turn the heat on the two burners to low, and using a spatula, work off those beautiful juices and chicken nubbins that have cooked onto the baking sheet. When it has all mixed well with the wine and the bottom of the baking sheet is freed of all chicken bits, divide the deglazing results evenly between the jars. Then evenly divide the onion, celery, carrots, tomato, thyme sprigs, peppercorns, coriander seeds, and bay leaves between the two jars. Fill each jar with cold water to just below the top and cap the jars with lids and bands so that they're finger-tight. Submerge the jars in the circulator water bath and cook for 5 hours, occasionally adding water if necessary to keep the jars submerged. (Or cover the bath with plastic wrap.)

6. Five minutes before the stock is ready, prepare an ice bath. We'll use it to shock and chill the stock for storage.

7. When the stock is ready, carefully remove the jars from the hot water bath (use a jar lifter if you have one, or tongs and a towel). Strain the stock through a fine-mesh strainer into a large container and discard the solids. Quickly and thoroughly clean the mason jars and pour the finished stock back into them. Leaving the jars uncovered, chill the stock in the ice bath for 10 minutes, until cool. Use within 4 days, or freeze for up to 6 months.

SHRIMP STOCK

Prep time: **10 minutes**

Cook time: **4 hours**

Circulator temperature
setting: **85°C / 185°F**

MAKES 2 TO 3 QUARTS

2 tablespoons canola oil

4 cups shrimp shells, patted dry

1 large yellow onion, diced

2 celery stalks, minced

3 garlic cloves, crushed

1 (1-inch) piece of fresh ginger, peeled and thinly sliced

2 tablespoons tomato paste

1 cup dry white wine (Sauvignon Blanc is great)

1 sprig fresh thyme

1 cup 1-inch pieces of fresh flat-leaf parsley stems

1 tablespoon coriander seeds, toasted

4 bay leaves

Pinch of crushed red pepper flakes

Shrimp shells and heads can produce a heady oceanic elixir of a stock to use as a base for so many things like complex stews, robust shrimp sauces, and brawny broths for seafood boils. It also freezes well, broadening the core elements of your larder. Even just a simple reduction of a shrimp stock with a squeeze of lemon and with some butter swirled in makes a terrific sauce for any kind of sautéed fish or pasta, and you can get creative from there.

1. Preheat the circulator water bath to 85°C / 185°F.

2. In a large skillet, heat the oil over high heat until it is nearly smoking. Add the shrimp shells and cook, stirring frequently, until they are pink and aromatic, about 4 minutes. Add the onion, celery, garlic, and ginger and cook until the vegetables have softened, another 4 minutes. Add the tomato paste and stir well to incorporate.

3. Remove the skillet from the heat and deglaze the pan with the white wine, loosening any scraps from the bottom of the skillet. Add the thyme sprigs, parsley stems, coriander seeds, bay leaves, and red pepper flakes and stir to incorporate.

4. Pour the contents of the skillet into two 2-quart mason jars, or divide it among smaller jars. Fill the jars with lukewarm water to 1 inch below the top. Cap each jar with a lid and band, tightening the bands to just finger-tight. Submerge the jars in the circulator water bath and cook for 4 hours, occasionally adding water if necessary to keep the jars submerged. (Or cover the bath with plastic wrap.)

5. Using a jar lifter or tongs and a towel, carefully remove the jars from the hot water bath. Strain the stock into a large container and discard the solids. Cool to room temperature. Clean the mason jars thoroughly, and then pour the stock back into the jars to store in the fridge. Use within 4 days, or freeze for up to 6 months.

BEEF STOCK

Prep time: **10 minutes**

Cook time: **30 minutes roasting, plus 8 hours**

Circulator temperature setting: **90°C / 194°F**

MAKES 2 TO
3 QUARTS

1 tablespoon vegetable oil

2 pounds beef leg or marrow bones, cut into 1-inch pieces (have the butcher do this)

1 yellow onion, cut into a large dice

1 large carrot, cut into 1-inch pieces

2 celery stalks, cut into 1-inch pieces

1 medium tomato, coarsely chopped

2 sprigs fresh thyme

2 bay leaves

4 garlic cloves

8 whole black peppercorns

Stocks made with bones are best made in wide-mouth two-quart mason jars, which will easily hold the bones. (A bone-punctured resealable bag is the worst.)

When I am shopping for beef bones, I often find the best ones at large Korean markets. Their butchers usually have inch-long cuts of leg bones or marrow bones, which have tons of flavor and body. I adore the H-Mart chain of Korean groceries, and there may be one near you, what with seventy-five stores (and counting) in North America.

1. Preheat the oven to 205°C / 400°F and preheat the circulator water bath to 90°C / 194°F.

2. Lightly oil a roasting pan with the vegetable oil and arrange the beef bones in the pan. Roast them in the oven, on the middle rack, for 30 minutes.

3. Remove the pan from the oven and carefully divide the bones between two 2-quart mason jars. Divide the onion, carrot, celery, and tomato equally between the jars. Add a thyme sprig, a bay leaf, 2 garlic cloves, and 4 peppercorns to each jar. Fill each jar with lukewarm water to 1 inch below the top. Cap each jar with a lid and band, tightening the band to just finger-tight. Submerge the jars in the circulator water bath and cook for 8 hours, occasionally adding water if necessary to keep the jars submerged. (Or cover the bath with plastic wrap.)

4. Using a jar lifter or tongs and a towel, carefully remove the jars from the hot water bath. Strain the stock into a large container and discard the bones and solids. Clean the mason jars thoroughly, and pour the strained stock back into them. Let the stock cool to room temperature, and then store it in the fridge and use it within 4 days, or freeze it for up to 6 months.

HAM STOCK

Prep time: **10 minutes**

Cook time: **30 minutes roasting, then 8 hours**

Circulator temperature setting: **90°C / 194°F**

MAKES 2 TO 3 QUARTS

1 **tablespoon** vegetable oil

2 **pounds** ham hocks, cut into 1-inch pieces (have the butcher do this)

1 medium yellow onion, cut into a large dice

1 large carrot, cut into 1-inch pieces

2 celery stalks, cut into 1-inch pieces

1 medium tomato, coarsely chopped

2 **sprigs** fresh thyme

2 bay leaves

4 garlic cloves

8 whole black peppercorns

I live in the South, and smoked ham hocks are pretty much a staple for us. If you don't live down here, you probably can find them at your local grocery and butcher shops, but you may just have to search a little more. They make a wonderful stock for a ton of uses, combining saltiness, smokiness, and rich umami. Use ham stock for anything from braised beans to risotto to a simple consommé to a base for a heartier dashi . . . the possibilities are quite endless.

1. Preheat the oven to 205°C /400°F and preheat the circulator water bath to 90°C / 194°F.

2. Lightly oil a roasting pan with the vegetable oil and arrange the ham hocks on the pan. Roast them in the oven, on the middle rack, for 30 minutes.

3. Remove the pan from the oven, and divide the ham hocks evenly between two 2-quart mason jars. Divide the onion, carrot, celery, and tomato equally between the jars. Add a thyme sprig, a bay leaf, 2 garlic cloves, and 4 peppercorns to each jar. Fill each jar with lukewarm water to 1 inch below the top and then cap the jar with a lid and band, tightening the band to just finger-tight. Submerge the jars in the circulator water bath and cook for 8 hours or as long as 12, occasionally adding water if necessary to keep the jars submerged. (Or cover the bath with plastic wrap.)

4. Using a jar lifter or tongs and a towel, carefully remove the jars from the hot water bath. Strain the stock into a large container and discard the bones and solids. Clean the mason jars thoroughly and pour the strained ham stock back into them. Let the stock cool to room temperature, and then store it in the fridge for up to 4 days, or freeze it for up to 6 months.

DASHI

Prep time: **2 minutes**

Cook time: **2¼ hours**

Circulator temperature setting: **85°C / 185°F**

MAKES 7 CUPS

2 ounces dried kombu

2 tablespoons dried bonito flakes

This makes a generous amount of dashi. Freeze it in 1-cup storage containers and be happy you have it on hand.

1. Preheat the circulator water bath to 85°C / 185°F.

2. Place the kombu in a clean 2-quart mason jar, one with a new lid and band, and pour in 1¾ quarts (7 cups) cold water. Cover with the lid and then tighten the band so that it's finger-tight.

3. Submerge the jar in the circulator water bath, with the water level a couple of inches below the top of the jar, and cook for 2 hours.

4. At the 2-hour mark, carefully remove the lid from the jar while it is still in the hot water bath and add the bonito flakes. Seal the jar once again and cook for 15 minutes more.

5. Using a jar lifter or tongs and some dexterity, carefully remove the jar from the water bath. Strain the dashi into a clean container. Use it immediately, or let it cool in the fridge, where it will keep for a couple of days. Or transfer the dashi to 1-cup containers and freeze them for up to 6 months.

CODDLED MAYO

Prep time: **5 minutes**

Cook time: **2 hours, plus 10 minutes finishing**

Circulator temperature setting: **58°C / 136.4°F**

MAKES 1 PINT

2 large eggs

1½ **teaspoons** Dijon mustard

2 garlic cloves, minced

1½ **tablespoons** freshly squeezed lemon juice

2 cups extra-virgin olive oil

Kosher salt

In the case of eggs, "coddle" means to cook an egg slowly, below the boiling point, to a safe temperature for eating. In an age of strange food-borne illnesses, it is a safe way to make things such as mayonnaise and Caesar dressing, aioli, and boiled dressing.

I live in the South, where your mayonnaise brand (Duke's or Hellmann's) is tribal and chosen by your elders, but I still believe homemade mayo reigns supreme.

1. Preheat the circulator water bath to 58°C / 136.4°F.

2. Using a slotted spoon, carefully lower the eggs directly into the circulator water bath. Cook for 2 hours.

3. Ten minutes before the eggs are finished cooking, prepare an ice bath.

4. Remove the eggs from the hot water bath and transfer them to the ice to shock them and stop the cooking. Let them cool in the ice bath for 5 minutes.

5. Crack the eggs into a small bowl, and then add the mustard, garlic, and lemon juice and whisk to blend. While whisking, slowly add the olive oil in a nice steady stream. Make sure not to add too much oil at once, or the emulsion may break. Once the oil is completely emulsified and the mayonnaise is smooth, season it with salt to taste, and with a final flourish, whisk to incorporate.

6. Store the coddled mayonnaise in an airtight container in the refrigerator. It will keep for 1 week.

CRÈME FRAÎCHE

Prep time: **5 minutes**

Cook time: **12 hours**

Circulator temperature setting: **40.6°C / 105°F**

MAKES 3½ CUPS

3 cups heavy cream
½ cup buttermilk

This recipe is meant to help you avoid a trip down yet another grocery aisle. Making this crème fraîche will also require the use of quart-size mason jars that you sink into the circulator bath. Crème fraîche plays the role of a super-rich sour cream in my kitchens, adding lusciousness to stock reductions, providing a base for soups, and working as a beginning to a salad dressing. It is also ridiculously expensive to buy ready-made, so make it yourself!

1. Preheat the circulator water bath to 40.6°C / 105°F.

2. Pour the heavy cream and buttermilk into a 1-quart mason jar. Cap the jar with a lid and band, tightening the band to just finger-tight. Submerge the jar in the circulator water bath and cook for 12 hours. Make sure the jar is completely submerged, and add water to maintain that level as necessary. (Or cover the bath with plastic wrap.)

3. Ten minutes before the crème fraîche is ready, prepare an ice bath.

4. Using a jar lifter or tongs and a towel, carefully remove the jar from the hot water bath and transfer it to the ice bath to cool. Once it has cooled, the crème fraîche is good to serve. If you're storing it, it will keep in the fridge for about 2 weeks.

STOCKS, SAUCES, ETC. **195**

SCRATCH YOGURT

Prep time: **10 minutes**

Cook time: **6 hours**

Circulator temperature setting: **43°C / 109 °F**

MAKES 1 QUART

1 quart whole milk

2 tablespoons plain whole-milk yogurt with live cultures

Great yogurt relies on great milk. Whole milk. Skim milk was created by the devil to lure us into some weird crossroads deal with sugar-laden cereals. I don't know this to be true, but I do know that I do not like skim milk.

Oh, but yogurt I love. It used to be made only by people whose names were Scout and Moonwonder, lived in communes, and milked their own goats. But those times have changed, and now we can live in the 'burbs, name our children Austin and SaraBeth, and buy great milk at the farmers' market. So go make some yogurt.

But first you must understand what yogurt is: Yogurt is a bacterial fermentation of milk. The good bacteria that causes the fermentation is a live lactic acid culture, which feeds on the milk and produces the thickness and the tartness. These good bacteria are also adept at crowding out bad bacteria, so the process of making yogurt, while seemingly scary to the uninitiated—purposely keeping milk warm for hours—is safe. Let us remember that food has been fermented for thousands of years. Bread, beer, wine, kimchi, hot sauce, pickles . . . all are fermented foods. So let that good bacteria flow! (Note: You need an instant-read thermometer for this.)

1. Preheat the circulator water bath to 43°C / 109°F.

2. In a large saucepan, heat the milk over medium heat until a thermometer placed in the center reads 82°C / 179.6°F. Then remove the pan from the heat and when the temperature has cooled to below 43°C / 109°F, whisk in the yogurt.

≫→ *Recipe continues*

3. Carefully transfer the milk-yogurt to a clean 1-quart mason jar. Cover the jar with its lid and tighten the band, and submerge the jar in the circulator water bath. (The water should reach all the way up to the top of the jar.) Cook for at least 6 hours—generally speaking, the longer it cooks, the tarter your yogurt will be. When it's done, it will be set and a bit custardy, like . . . yogurt. But for a more sour-tasting yogurt, you can leave it cooking for 8, 12, or even 24 hours. Cover the bath with plastic wrap to prevent you from having to check and refill the water all the time.

4. Using a jar lifter or tongs and a towel, carefully remove the jar from the hot water bath and set it on the counter. Remove the lid and let the yogurt cool to room temperature. Then reseal the jar and store it in the fridge. The yogurt will stay fresh in the fridge for 1 week, or for a month if you are Francis Lam, my editor.

SMALL-BATCH TOMATO SAUCE

Prep time: **5 minutes**

Cook time: **I hour**

Circulator temperature setting: **85°C / 185°F**

MAKES 1 QUART

2 pounds mixed fresh tomatoes, such as vine-ripe and cherry heirlooms

½ sweet yellow onion, cut into a large dice

3 garlic cloves

2 tablespoons unsalted butter

1 tablespoon extra-virgin olive oil

8 fresh basil leaves

2 sprigs fresh thyme

Kosher salt and freshly ground black pepper

Sure, you can cook tomato sauce in a pan. But the first time you walk away and scorch it, you will see the beauty of a recipe where you can walk away and return hours later to a radical success. This is a mother sauce, meant for pastas and meatballs, eggplant and stewed zucchini—wherever you need a good tomato sauce.

1. Preheat the circulator water bath to 85°C / 185°F.

2. Place the tomatoes, onion, garlic, butter, olive oil, basil, thyme sprigs, and a few pinches of salt and pepper in a resealable gallon-size plastic bag and seal the bag using the displacement method (see page 17). Submerge the bag in the circulator water bath and cook for 1 hour. (You can also cook it in a clean mason jar with the top screwed on finger-tight.)

3. Remove the bag from the hot water bath and discard the thyme sprigs. Carefully transfer the contents of the bag to a food processor or blender. Purée for 30 seconds, or until the sauce reaches the desired chunkiness. (I like mine mostly smooth.) Season with additional salt and pepper to taste.

4. Serve with your favorite pasta or store in the fridge in a mason jar. It will keep for 5 days.

LONG-COOK SALSA

Prep time: **45 minutes**

Cook time: **I hour**

Circulator temperature setting: **80°C / 176°F**

MAKES 1 QUART

1 poblano pepper

½ teaspoon vegetable oil

10 Roma tomatoes, cored and cut into ½-inch dice

2 garlic cloves, minced

1 teaspoon chili powder

½ teaspoon freshly ground cumin seeds

1 shallot, minced

1 teaspoon kosher salt

1 tablespoon freshly squeezed lime juice

2 tablespoons minced fresh cilantro leaves

This is a simple salsa that will up your chips-and-salsa game. Jarred salsa always tastes like a jar to me. This one, on the other hand, tastes like a beautiful marriage of tomatoes and chiles, as salsa is supposed to taste. The added bonus is that it freezes well in small batches.

1. Preheat the oven to 220°C / 425°F, and preheat the circulator water bath to 80°C / 176°F.

2. Place the poblano pepper, whole, in a cast-iron skillet and drizzle it with the vegetable oil. Place the skillet in the preheated oven and roast the pepper for about 15 minutes, turning occasionally, until softened and browned in spots.

3. Remove the skillet from the oven and transfer the pepper to a bowl. Cover the bowl with plastic wrap and let the poblano sit for 15 minutes.

4. When the poblano is cool enough to handle, work the skin away from the flesh with your fingers or with a paper towel. Slice the pepper in half lengthwise, and discard the stem and seeds. Finely mince the pepper flesh and transfer it to a large bowl. Add the tomatoes, garlic, chili powder, cumin, shallot, and salt and stir to combine.

5. Place the salsa in a resealable gallon-size plastic bag and seal the bag using the displacement method (see page 17). Submerge the bag in the circulator water bath and cook for 1 hour. (You can also cook it in a large clean mason jar with the top screwed on finger-tight.)

6. Remove the bag from the hot water bath and carefully empty the contents into a large bowl. Add the lime juice and cilantro and stir to incorporate. Cover the bowl with plastic wrap and chill the salsa in the fridge before serving. Pack it up into a clean mason jar if you want to eat it later in the week, or grab some chips and dig in right away.

This chapter is huge, but with good reason: The way we eat has changed so much in the past decade. We are finally giving center-of-the-plate focus to the vegetables and fruits of the world. This has happened for a panoply of reasons, from health awareness, to economics and the high price of quality for meat-based meals, to concerns about sustainability in our farming systems. But to me, the most wonderful reason is a simple one: We finally learned how to cook vegetables well.

Most vegetables don't need to be boiled to achieve a wonderful cooked state. Most of the recipes here cook at around 85°C (185°F), with the times being pretty important to keep the vegetables in a nice state of crunch or thoroughly tender, depending on the recipe. That said, you can often cook many vegetables at the same time if the temperature in all those recipes is the same. The cooking times will be the only variable to look out for, and then we finish them with flavor-packed setups. All the more reason to make an elaborate vegetable plate for dinner that much more often.

Go on, eat your veggies. It is a better time than ever to do it.

CELERY ROOT PURÉE

Prep time: **10 minutes**

Cook time: **1½ hours, plus 5 minutes finishing**

Circulator temperature setting: **85°C / 185°F**

SERVES 4 AS A SIDE

2 cups diced celery root (from 1 large root, peeled)

1 cup whole milk

1 bay leaf

½ teaspoon kosher salt

2 tablespoons cold unsalted butter, cubed

Celery root, or celeriac, is such a naturally smooth and luscious purée when you cook it right. A sweeter, familiar-but-intriguing cousin of mashed potatoes, this side dish is straightforward and pairs well with just about anything, but it has an intimate culinary relationship with most fine pork and poultry dishes. It reheats well, too. This is one of those recipes that you can cook for a while past the prescribed time, holding it hot in the water bath until you're ready to purée and serve, and it will be fine. This will pair perfectly with the Duck Confit (page 100).

1. Preheat the circulator water bath to 85°C / 185°F.

2. Place the celery root, milk, bay leaf, and salt in a resealable gallon-size plastic bag and seal it using the displacement method (see page 17). Submerge the bag in the circulator water bath and cook for 1½ hours, until the celery root feels really, really tender. At this point you can hold it hot in the bath until you're ready to purée and serve.

3. Transfer the celery root and the cooking milk to a blender (discard the bay leaf) and purée on medium speed. While the blender is running, add the butter and purée until completely smooth.

4. Serve immediately or chill and store in a sealed container in the fridge for up to a week.

BREAD-AND-BUTTER PICKLES

Prep time: **30 minutes**

Cook time: **15 minutes**

Circulator temperature
setting: **82°C / 179.6°F**

MAKES 1 QUART

4 **cups** thinly sliced English
cucumbers (about 2 cucumbers;
sliced ⅛ inch thick)

½ **cup** thinly sliced yellow onion

¼ **cup** minced celery stalks,
with leaves

2 **tablespoons** kosher salt

¼ **cup** light brown sugar

½ **teaspoon** whole cloves

½ **teaspoon** ground turmeric

4 allspice berries

½ **teaspoon** celery seeds

1 **cup** cider vinegar

Bread-and-butter pickles are the classic sweet-tart pickle of
the American larder, and this recipe is so dang easy that
there is no reason not to make them from scratch, keeping
their texture snappy and their flavors fresh. Enjoy them on a
burger, in a sandwich, or eat them on their own the way we
do in the South, where we are a pickle plate culture.

1. Preheat the circulator water bath to 82°C / 179.6°F.

2. In a resealable gallon-size plastic bag, combine
the cucumbers, onion, celery, salt, brown sugar, cloves,
turmeric, allspice berries, celery seeds, cider vinegar, and
1 cup of water. Seal the bag using the displacement method
(see page 17). Submerge the bag in the circulator water bath
and cook for 15 minutes.

3. Five minutes before the cooking time has elapsed,
prepare an ice bath.

4. Remove the bag from the hot water bath, immediately
plunge it into the ice bath. and let the pickles cool. When
they are cool enough to handle, carefully pour the contents
of the bag into a clean glass jar.

5. Store the pickles in a tightly covered jar in the fridge for
up to a month.

CARA CARA ORANGE MARMALADE

Prep time: **45 minutes**

Cook time: **4 hours, plus 20 minutes finishing**

Circulator temperature setting: **85°C / 185°F**

MAKES 2 QUARTS

12 medium oranges (baseball-size)

1 lemon

4 cups sugar

1 tablespoon kosher salt

2 teaspoons instant powdered pectin

I have always been on very friendly terms with marmalade. It has a savory charm at the beginning, a sweet middle, and a refreshing yet bitter finish. In the morning, I like marmalade with well-toasted seeded bread and the accommodating luxury of unsalted butter. At lunch, it can adorn a turkey sandwich with crisp lettuce, sliced avocado, and a generous amount of freshly ground black pepper. For dinner, the marmalade will make a wonderful condiment for pork loin or be an integral balance to a buttermilk panna cotta. It is a great thing to have in your arsenal and will stay fresh in the fridge for up to three weeks. You can also fully can it if you'd like, in which case it will be shelf-stable for a year; just follow the canning instructions provided by the jar manufacturer.

So why cook marmalade à la sous vide? Because it means a long cook time without the possibility of scorching the fruit. It means concentrating the flavors without losing a lot of volume to evaporation. The final step is to transfer the marmalade to a pot and bring it to a boil, or 212°F, which is the temperature which pectin need to hit to set.

The key is to make a good choice of citrus. I love the pink hue of Cara Cara oranges or the simplicity of a really fresh navel. Stick to seedless and you will speed up the process a lot. This is a very classic recipe, but you can alter it here and there. Mint, ground black pepper, Aleppo pepper, lemon verbena . . . there are many options to explore.

1. Preheat the circulator water bath to 85°C / 185°F.

2. Using a sharp vegetable peeler, remove all the orange and lemon zest in strips, trying to take as little white pith as possible. Stack the strips of zest into piles on a cutting board and slice them, using a sharp chef's knife, into very narrow matchstick lengths.

⟫➤ *Recipe continues*

3. Cut a ¼-inch-thick slice off the top and bottom of the lemon and each orange. Then, using a sharp paring knife, cut away the pith, following the curve of the citrus all the way around while leaving the inner flesh intact.

4. Once the pith has been discarded, cut the flesh into ½-inch pieces and place them in a large bowl. Add the zest, sugar, and salt and toss well. Place the citrus mixture in a resealable gallon-size plastic bag and seal it using the displacement method (see page 17). Submerge the bag in the circulator water bath and cook for 4 hours.

5. Remove the bag from the hot water bath and pour the citrus mixture into a large saucepan. Add the pectin and stir to combine. Place the saucepan over high heat and bring the mixture to a boil to activate the pectin. Then reduce the heat to a simmer and cook for 15 minutes.

6. Five minutes before the marmalade is ready, prepare an ice bath.

7. Remove the saucepan from the heat, carefully transfer the marmalade to clean glass jars, and set the jars, uncovered, in the ice bath to cool. (You have to transfer it into the jars while it's hot, lest it set while cooling.)

8. Cover the jars and store the marmalade in the fridge. (You can also fully can the marmalade by following the jar manufacturer's instructions. Marmalade is high-acid, so water-bath canning is fine.)

STEWED PLANTAINS

Prep time: **10 minutes**

Cook time: **30 minutes, plus 10 minutes finishing**

Circulator temperature setting: **85°C / 185°F**

SERVES 4 AS A SIDE

4 mid-ripe plantains, cut diagonally into ¼-inch-thick slices

3 tablespoons cold unsalted butter, cubed

2 tablespoons light brown sugar

1 teaspoon ground cinnamon

1 cardamom pod, cracked

1 teaspoon kosher salt

1 bay leaf

Plantains are so much more than a banana. They are the savory or sweet bounty of the Caribbean. This dish is akin to the plantains served at one of my favorite restaurants of all time, Kelly's Jamaican Food, in the charming city that I call home, Athens, Georgia.

The plantains you use for this recipe should be mid-ripe, meaning yellow, just turning brown. The bright green ones are unripe and the black ones are total bombs of sugar. All have their place in the culinary world, but for this dish you want the plantain to still have enough starch to serve it as a side to a piece of spicy grilled meat or a rich braise like Ropa Vieja (page 127), while packing some sweetness and tropical aromas.

1. Preheat the circulator water bath to 85°C / 185°F.

2. Place the plantains, butter, brown sugar, cinnamon, cardamom pod, salt, and bay leaf in a resealable gallon-size plastic bag and seal it using the displacement method (see page 17). Submerge the bag in the circulator water bath (make sure the plantains are fully submerged) and cook for 30 minutes.

3. Remove the bag from the hot water bath and carefully transfer the contents to a large skillet, fishing out the cardamom pod and the bay leaf. Cook over medium-high heat, stirring occasionally, until the liquid has reduced, and the plantains are evenly glazed, about 5 minutes. Serve.

SOUTHERN CHOW-CHOW

Prep time: **30 minutes, plus 2 hours marinating**

Cook time: **4 hours**

Circulator temperature setting: **85°C / 185°F**

MAKES 1 QUART

- ½ **cup** finely chopped green cabbage
- ½ **cup** finely chopped cauliflower
- ½ **cup** peeled and minced celery
- ½ **cup** diced green tomatoes (½-inch dice)
- ½ **cup** finely diced red bell peppers
- ¼ **cup** minced sweet onion
- ¼ **cup** minced scallions
- 1 **tablespoon** minced fresh ginger
- 1 **tablespoon** kosher salt
- ½ **cup** cider vinegar
- 2 **tablespoons** sugar
- 1 **teaspoon** yellow mustard seeds
- 1 **teaspoon** dried mustard
- 1 **teaspoon** celery seeds
- ½ **teaspoon** ground cumin
- ½ **teaspoon** ground turmeric
- 1 **teaspoon** chili powder

Chow-chow is a spicy, vinegary relish and a staple of the put-ups world. (*Put-ups* is Southern slang for *preserves and pickles*.) The core ingredients of cabbage, bell peppers, and green tomatoes seem to appear in the garden at the same time of year, and I am sure that this condiment was created to deal with the harvest. Chow-chow has a complex, almost Indian spice component to it, and you could add some heat if you like things on the fiery side. You can also add other things that are growing out of control in your garden, like pickling cucumbers or summer squash. The relatively high cooking temperature breaks it all down into a wonderful condiment, a graceful accompaniment to all sorts of meals. And the beauty of the long cook time is that you can just get it going and walk away.

1. Preheat the circulator water bath to 85°C / 185°F.

2. In a large bowl, combine the cabbage, cauliflower, celery, green tomato, bell pepper, sweet onion, scallions, and ginger. Add the salt, mix thoroughly, and let sit for 2 hours at room temperature.

3. Drain off and discard the liquid that the salt has pulled out of the vegetables. Reserve the strained vegetables in the large mixing bowl and add the vinegar, sugar, mustard seeds, dry mustard, celery seeds, cumin, turmeric, and chili powder. Stir to combine.

4. Place the ingredients in a resealable gallon-size plastic bag and seal it using the displacement method (see page 17). Submerge the bag in the circulator water bath and cook for 4 hours, checking to see if you need to add more water after a couple of hours. (Or cover the bath with plastic wrap.)

5. Five minutes before the chow-chow is ready, prepare an ice bath.

6. Remove the bag from the hot water bath and submerge it in the ice bath for about 15 minutes to cool.

7. Transfer the chow-chow to clean jars, seal, and store in the fridge. The chow-chow will stay fresh for up to 2 weeks.

LEEKS BARIGOULE

with Prosciutto and Shaved Parmesan

Prep time: 15 minutes

Cook time: 45 minutes, plus 6 minutes finishing

Circulator temperature setting: 85°C / 185°F

SERVES 4 AS A SIDE

4 medium leeks (white and light green parts only), rinsed well to remove any grit from between the leaves

¼ **cup** dry white wine

¼ **cup** white wine vinegar

¼ **cup** chicken stock (page 188) or vegetable stock (page 187)

½ lemon, thinly sliced

2 **tablespoons** fresh tarragon leaves

1 bay leaf

1 sprig fresh thyme

2 **tablespoons** cold unsalted butter, cubed

Kosher salt and freshly ground black pepper

2 **tablespoons** extra-virgin olive oil, plus more for finishing

4 slices prosciutto, torn into ⅛-inch-wide pieces

¼ **cup** shaved Parmesan cheese

¼ **cup** fresh flat-leaf parsley leaves

Barigoule usually refers to artichokes braised until tender, absorbing the flavors of white wine and olive oil, often served with some type of cured ham. This recipe follows the same method but uses leeks instead of artichokes. Leeks are the king of the large allium family, a sweet and redolent gift from the garden. You could make this as an accompaniment to a larger meal, or serve it as an appetizer, or even make it a light summer meal with some crusty bread and salumi on the side.

1. Preheat the circulator water bath to 85°C / 185°F.

2. Combine the leeks, white wine, vinegar, chicken stock, lemon slices, tarragon leaves, bay leaf, thyme sprig, butter, a pinch each of salt and pepper, and the 2 tablespoons olive oil in a resealable gallon-size plastic bag and seal it using the displacement method (see page 17). Submerge the bag in the circulator water bath and cook for 45 minutes.

3. Remove the bag from the hot water bath and carefully transfer the leeks to a cutting board, reserving the poaching liquid in the plastic bag or in a small bowl.

4. Slice the leeks into ½-inch-thick rounds. Heat a thin film of olive oil in a large cast-iron skillet over medium-high heat. When the oil begins to shimmer, add the leeks and cook for 4 minutes, flipping them halfway through, to brown. Transfer the leeks to a platter, reserving the skillet, and set them aside.

5. Raise the heat under the skillet to high. Add the reserved poaching liquid and cook until it is heated through, about 1 minute.

6. To serve, spoon ¼ cup of the warmed poaching liquid over the leeks. Top with the torn prosciutto, shaved Parmesan, and parsley. Season with additional salt to taste, and serve immediately.

DASHI-BRAISED TURNIPS

Finished in Butter and Soy

SERVES 4 AS A SIDE

1 pound small turnips (Hakurei, aka Tokyo turnips, would be best; the turnips should be no bigger than a golf ball), cut into large bite-size pieces

1 cup Dashi (page 193)

2 tablespoons unsalted butter

1½ teaspoons kosher salt

2 tablespoons light soy sauce

1 tablespoon sesame seeds, toasted

Dashi is the sea-based mother stock of Japanese cooking, a delicate and familiar flavor that is a foundation for many dishes. It is a great cooking medium and in this case melds with the sweetness of turnips, richness of butter, and depth of soy sauce to make a stellar side dish.

You won't be using the greens from the turnips in this recipe, so cut them off and immerse them in cold water to dislodge any dirt. Dry the greens and pack them up to use for something else—an easy braise in dashi until tender, finished with some lemon, would be a great idea.

1. Preheat the circulator water bath to 85°C / 185°F.

2. Combine the turnips, dashi, 1 tablespoon of the butter, and 1 teaspoon of the salt in a resealable gallon-size plastic bag and seal it using the displacement method (see page 17). Submerge the bag in the circulator water bath and cook for 30 minutes.

3. Remove the bag from the hot water bath and strain the turnips over a bowl. Discard the cooking liquid, or use it to cook those greens you saved.

4. Heat the remaining 1 tablespoon butter in a large stainless-steel skillet over medium heat. When the butter begins to froth, add the strained turnips and the soy sauce and cook, turning the turnips over once or twice as they cook, until they begin to color, about 4 minutes. Add the sesame seeds, toss to evenly distribute them, and transfer the turnips to a platter. Season with the remaining ½ teaspoon salt and serve immediately.

STEWED TOMATOES

Prep time: **20 minutes**

Cook time: **2 hours**

Circulator temperature
setting: **85°C / 185°F**

MAKES 2 QUARTS

3 pounds large heirloom tomatoes

2 celery stalks, cut into 1-inch pieces

½ sweet yellow onion, diced

1 cup vegetable stock (page 187),
chicken stock (page 188), or water

2 tablespoons extra-virgin olive oil

2 fresh basil leaves

2 teaspoons kosher salt

If you grow tomatoes, you know that you can get a sudden abundance of fruit that ripens fast. This recipe is based on a simple canning-style "put up" of tomatoes. The stewed tomatoes can be eaten straight up or canned in mason jars for eating throughout the year. The use of sous vide will make the tomatoes taste very fresh, cooked but still bright and sweet, because we are not cooking them down. The key here is to get beautiful ripe tomatoes. Puréed, this makes a simple soup, but I also like it just spooned over rice with some chicken and herbs. Simple eating can be some of the most special eating.

1. Preheat the circulator water bath to 85°C / 185°F.

2. Bring a large pot of water to a boil. In a large bowl, prepare an ice bath.

3. With a small kitchen knife, score an "X" on the bottom of each tomato. Carefully place the tomatoes in the boiling water and blanch for 30 to 60 seconds, until their skins begin to loosen. Transfer them to the ice bath to stop the cooking.

4. When the tomatoes are cool enough to handle, peel them and discard the skins. Cut the peeled tomatoes into quarters.

5. Place the tomatoes, celery, onion, stock, olive oil, basil leaves, and salt in a resealable gallon-size plastic bag and seal it using the displacement method (see page 17). Submerge the bag in the circulator water bath, ensuring that the tomatoes are under the water, and cook for 2 hours.

6. Remove the bag from the hot water bath and transfer the stewed tomatoes to a bowl. Serve 'em up with some steamed rice and hot sauce, or pack them up to use later. They will stay fresh in the fridge for up to a week.

BRUSSELS SPROUTS

with Bacon, Lemon, and Parsley

Prep time: **20 minutes**

Cook time: **30 minutes, plus 5 minutes finishing**

Circulator temperature setting: **85°C / 185°F**

SERVES 4 AS A SIDE

¼ **pound** slab smoked bacon, cut into a fine julienne

4 **cups** Brussels sprouts, cut in half from top to bottom

½ **teaspoon** freshly grated lemon zest

1 **teaspoon** kosher salt

2 **tablespoons** extra-virgin olive oil

½ **cup** fresh flat-leaf parsley leaves, minced

In this recipe, the Brussels sprouts poach in bacon fat, and then you give the sprouts some charred texture and flavor once they come out of the bag. It is a delicious treatment for this formerly shunned brassica.

1. Preheat the circulator water bath to 85°C / 185°F.

2. Place a cast-iron skillet over medium heat and add the bacon. Cook for 5 minutes, or until the bacon is crisp. Turn off the heat and let the bacon and its rendered fat cool in the pan.

3. When the bacon and bacon fat have cooled, transfer both to a resealable gallon-size plastic bag (reserve the skillet). Add the Brussels sprouts, lemon zest, and salt, and seal the bag using the displacement method (see page 17). Submerge the bag in the circulator water bath and cook for 30 minutes.

4. About 5 minutes before the Brussels sprouts are ready, prepare an ice bath.

5. Remove the bag from the hot water bath and plunge it into the ice water to flash-chill, stopping the cooking.

6. Return the cast-iron skillet to medium-high heat. When it is very hot, add the olive oil. When the oil is shimmering, add the contents of the bag, spread out in a single layer, and cook for 5 minutes, stirring occasionally, until the Brussels sprouts have charred in spots. Stir in the parsley and transfer everything to a dish. Serve them up to hungry people.

EGGPLANT

with Mirin, Ginger, and Soy

Prep time: **10 minutes**

Cook time: **45 minutes, plus 5 minutes finishing**

Circulator temperature setting: **85°C / 185°F**

SERVES 4 AS A SIDE

- **4** Japanese eggplants, cut in half lengthwise (globe eggplants will work fine as well, but cut those into ½-inch-thick rounds)
- **3 tablespoons** mirin (sweet rice wine for cooking)
- **2 tablespoons** minced fresh ginger (from a thick 2-inch piece)
- **2 tablespoons** soy sauce
- **1 teaspoon** kosher salt, plus more to taste
- **2 tablespoons** extra-virgin olive oil
- **2 tablespoons** thinly sliced fresh scallions, white and light green parts only
- **1 teaspoon** sesame seeds, toasted

This way of cooking eggplant has always struck me as counterintuitive, because usually eggplant is seared first or cooked whole, but in this case, it is cooked with the punchy flavors of soy, mirin, and ginger and then drained and seared, to wonderful results. I started making this at home years ago, and it has been a standard weekly offering ever since.

1. Preheat the circulator water bath to 85°C / 185°F.

2. Place the eggplant halves, mirin, ginger, soy sauce, and 1 teaspoon salt in a resealable gallon-size plastic bag and seal it using the displacement method (see page 17). Submerge the bag in the circulator water bath and cook for 45 minutes.

3. Remove the bag from the hot water bath and transfer the eggplant to a plate lined with paper towels. Discard the bag and the cooking liquid. Pat the eggplant dry.

4. Heat the olive oil in a large nonstick or cast-iron skillet over medium-high heat. When the oil starts to shimmer, add the eggplant, cut-side down, to the skillet. Sear the eggplant in the skillet for 4 minutes, or until you've achieved a nice golden-brown color.

5. To serve, arrange the eggplant halves on a small platter and garnish with the sliced scallions and toasted sesame seeds. Season with salt to taste.

BEETS, PISTACHIOS, TARRAGON,

and Ricotta Salata

Prep time: **20 minutes**

Cook time: **30 minutes**

Circulator temperature
setting: **85°C / 185°F**

SERVES 4 TO 6
AS A SIDE

3 pounds beets (golf-ball size), peeled
and halved

2 teaspoons kosher salt

1 tablespoon honey

2 teaspoons sherry vinegar

2 sprigs fresh thyme

¼ **cup** extra-virgin olive oil

3 tablespoons fresh tarragon leaves

¼ **cup** chopped roasted pistachios

¼ **cup** thinly shaved dry ricotta
salata

1 tablespoon torn fresh mint leaves

Modernist salad-type thing alert: This may seem like a
totally random combination, but these flavors work really
well together. I do think tarragon is an unsung partner
to vegetables; I adore pistachios; and ricotta salata has a
beautiful saline kick. The beets should be on the small end
of the size spectrum for the time allotted for cooking, but
if you happen to be using big ones, just add to the cooking
time to compensate.

1. Preheat the circulator water bath to 85°C / 185°F.

2. Place the beets, salt, honey, sherry vinegar, thyme
sprigs, olive oil, and 2 tablespoons of the tarragon in a
resealable gallon-size plastic bag and seal it using the
displacement method (see page 17). Submerge the bag in the
circulator water bath and cook for 30 minutes.

3. Remove the bag from the hot water bath and let it cool.
Remove the beets from the bag and set them aside, reserving
the braising liquid in the bag.

4. Strain the braising liquid through a fine-mesh strainer
into a separate container and set it aside. (You'll use some of
it to dress the beets.) Discard the solids.

5. To serve, arrange the beets on a nice wide plate. Spoon
2 tablespoons of the reserved cooking liquid over the beets,
then top them with the chopped pistachios and shaved
ricotta salata. Garnish with the torn mint and remaining
1 tablespoon tarragon leaves. Serve immediately.

MUSHY PEAS

with Shallots and Mint

Prep time: **20 minutes**

Cook time: **45 minutes, plus 5 minutes finishing**

Circulator temperature setting: **85°C / 185°F**

SERVES 4 AS A SIDE

- **2 cups** fresh English peas (frozen peas will work fine in a pinch)
- **1** shallot, minced
- **1 tablespoon** freshly grated lemon zest
- **2 tablespoons** unsalted butter
- **¼ cup** chicken stock (page 188) or vegetable stock (page 187)
- Kosher salt and freshly ground black pepper
- **2 tablespoons** fresh mint leaves, sliced

The past twenty years have seen a rebirth in British food, losing the generalized reputation of bland, overcooked, and uninspired. The funny thing is that, although the food scene in England is truly exciting and international, technical and packed with flavor, I actually adore some of the historical recipes that represent the old guard of British food—including roast beef, Yorkshire pudding, and mushy peas. This is a modern take on the latter, with plenty of lemon aroma, and you can serve it up with whatever you like. It is a beauty of a recipe.

1. Preheat the circulator water bath to 85°C / 185°F.

2. Place the peas, shallot, lemon zest, butter, chicken stock, and a pinch each of salt and pepper in a resealable gallon-size plastic bag and seal it using the displacement method (see page 17). Submerge the bag in the circulator water bath and cook for 45 minutes.

3. Remove the bag from the hot water bath and transfer the contents to a food processor. Pulse, being careful not to overwork the peas, and season with salt and pepper to taste. You're not looking for a purée—they are called mushy peas after all. (If you don't have a food processor, you can use a potato masher to mash the peas.)

4. Spoon the peas onto a plate or into a large bowl. Garnish with the mint leaves and serve.

ACORN SQUASH

with Pumpkin Seed Salsa, Chocolate, and Queso Fresco

Prep time: **10 minutes**

Cook time: **30 minutes, plus 10 minutes finishing**

Circulator temperature setting: **85°C / 185°F**

SERVES 4 AS A SIDE

2 acorn squash, halved vertically, seeded, and cut into ½-inch-thick slices

2 **tablespoons** cold unsalted butter, cubed

1 **teaspoon** light brown sugar

Kosher salt and freshly ground black pepper

½ **cup** roasted pumpkin seeds, chopped

¼ **cup** fresh mint leaves, chopped

¼ **cup** fresh flat-leaf parsley leaves, chopped

¼ **cup** freshly squeezed lime juice (about 3 limes)

¼ **cup** extra-virgin olive oil

2 **tablespoons** queso fresco

1 **ounce** dark chocolate

This recipe sounds wackier than it is. I grew up with my father concocting pretty good acorn squash sides with some maple syrup and butter, cooked in the *microwave*. Always ahead of the curve, my dad: a single father, a busy professor, and the owner of the first microwave in our neighborhood. All of these attributes contributed to his squash method.

This recipe is very modern in style, so get some tweezers, some skinny jeans, some emo music, and get cooking.

1. Preheat the circulator water bath to 85°C / 185°F.

2. Place the squash slices, butter, brown sugar, and a pinch each of salt and pepper in a resealable gallon-size plastic bag and seal it using the displacement method (see page 17). Submerge the bag in the circulator water bath and cook for 30 minutes.

3. In a small bowl, combine the pumpkin seeds, mint, parsley, lime juice, and 2 tablespoons of the olive oil. Season with a pinch each of salt and pepper. Gently whisk to combine the salsa.

4. Remove the bag from the hot water bath and transfer the squash to a plate lined with paper towels. Pat the squash dry to remove any excess liquid.

5. Heat the remaining 2 tablespoons olive oil in a large skillet over medium-high heat. When the oil begins to shimmer, add the squash slices and sear until they are nice and caramelized, about 3 minutes per side.

6. To serve, arrange the squash on a platter and spoon the salsa on top. Garnish with crumbles of queso fresco. Use a Microplane to grate the dark chocolate over the dish—don't be shy with it. Eat!

CABBAGE
with Walnuts and Parmesan

Prep time: **5 minutes**

Cook time: **45 minutes, plus 10 minutes finishing**

Circulator temperature setting: **85°C / 185°F**

SERVES 4 AS A SIDE

1 medium head green cabbage (about 2 pounds), trimmed and quartered

4 tablespoons (½ stick) cold unsalted butter, cubed

2 tablespoons cider vinegar

1 teaspoon nigella seeds, toasted (caraway seeds work in a pinch)

Kosher salt

1 lemon, cut into wedges

Toasted unsalted walnuts, for garnishing

¼ cup shaved Parmesan cheese

This is one that you can make a few days in advance and store in the fridge before crisping in the pan. It's a great side. I like to eat this by itself sometimes, though—it's that good. Cooking the cabbage sous vide lets you cook it down until tender without any of the boiling-cabbage stink. Eat as a warm salad or serve alongside Corned Beef (page 137).

1. Preheat the circulator water bath to 85°C / 185°F.

2. Place the cabbage quarters, 2 tablespoons of the butter, the vinegar, the nigella seeds, and a pinch of salt in a resealable gallon-size plastic bag and seal it using the displacement method (see page 17), Submerge the bag in the circulator water bath and cook for 45 minutes.

3. Ten minutes before the cabbage is ready, prepare an ice bath.

4. Remove the bag from the hot water bath and plunge it into the ice bath to cool. (Once cooled, the sous vide cabbage will keep in the refrigerator in the bag for 4 days. You can complete these next steps when you're ready to serve it.)

5. When you're ready to eat, take the cabbage out of the bag and place it on a cutting board. Pat the cabbage dry with a paper towel to remove any excess liquid.

6. Heat the remaining 2 tablespoons butter in a large skillet over medium heat. When the butter begins to froth, add the cabbage quarters, cut-side down, and sear them for 3 minutes on each cut side, or until the cabbage is nicely browned and beginning to char. Season with salt to taste.

7. To serve, transfer the cabbage quarters to individual plates. Squeeze 1 lemon wedge over each cabbage quarter, and then garnish each cabbage quarter by grating the walnuts over them as you would cheese. Top with the shaved Parmesan and season with salt to taste.

LEMON-BUTTER GRILLED ARTICHOKES

Prep time: **30 minutes**

Cook time: **I hour, plus 5 minutes finishing**

Circulator temperature setting: **85°C / 185°F**

SERVES 4

4 large globe artichokes

1 lemon, halved

1 tablespoon freshly grated lemon zest

6 tablespoons (¾ stick) cold unsalted butter, cubed

Kosher salt and freshly ground black pepper

1 tablespoon extra-virgin olive oil

2 cups crème fraîche (page 195) or coddled mayonnaise (page 194)

I grew up with steamed artichokes. We were living south of San Francisco and Dad was teaching at Stanford and I was two years old. I don't remember much, but I remember whole steamed artichokes and handmade egg rolls, the swimming pool, and the driveway. Everything else is a blur, but the artichokes never faded from my list of favorite foods. This is a simple way to serve them, not without some labor and prep at the beginning, but worth every bit of it. The results are amazing.

1. Preheat the circulator water bath to 85°C / 185°F.

2. To clean the artichokes, fill a large mixing bowl about half full with water, and squeeze one of the lemon halves into the water.

3. Cut off the top ¼ inch of the first artichoke. Peel away the tough outer leaves and discard them. Cut ⅛ inch off the bottom of the stem. Using a vegetable peeler, peel away the outer layer of the stem.

4. With a heavy kitchen knife, cut the artichoke in half lengthwise, and then cut away the very center (the hairy "choke") of the artichoke. Place the artichoke in the bowl of acidulated water, and repeat for the remaining 3 artichokes. Once the artichokes are cleaned, remove them from the acidulated water and pat them dry with a paper towel.

5. Place the artichokes, the juice of the remaining lemon half, the lemon zest, the butter, and a pinch each of salt and pepper in a resealable gallon-size plastic bag and seal it using the displacement method (see page 17). Submerge the bag in the circulator water bath and cook for 1 hour, or until the artichokes are tender.

6. About 10 minutes before the artichokes are done, either get your grill going (you will need it to reach 400°F) or preheat your broiler to medium or high.

7. Remove the bag from the hot water bath and transfer the artichokes to a baking sheet. Brush the artichokes with the olive oil and grill (or broil) them for about 2 minutes per side, until golden brown. Serve immediately with the crème fraîche or some coddled mayo for dipping.

WHITE ASPARAGUS

with Poached Egg and Onion Soubise

Prep time: **20 minutes**

Cook time: **15 minutes, plus 5 minutes finishing**

Circulator temperature setting: **85°C / 185°F**

SERVES 2 AS A LIGHT MEAL OR 4 AS AN APPETIZER OR SIDE

2 pounds fresh white asparagus

1 tablespoon freshly grated lemon zest

1 sprig fresh thyme

2 tablespoons unsalted butter

1 tablespoon extra-virgin olive oil

1 cup Onion Soubise (page 269)

4 freshly poached 63.5°C Eggs (page 103)

Kosher salt and freshly ground black pepper

2 tablespoons freshly grated Parmesan cheese

1 tablespoon minced fresh chives

Half-slice of lemon, for serving

Soubise and egg. Classic pairing.
Egg and asparagus. Also a classic pairing.
All together? Truly awesome.

1. Preheat the circulator water bath to 85°C / 185°F.

2. Place the asparagus, lemon zest, thyme sprig, and butter in a resealable gallon-size plastic bag and seal it using the displacement method (see page 17). Submerge the bag in the circulator water bath and cook for 15 minutes.

3. Remove the bag from the hot water bath and set it aside. Remove the asparagus from the bag and pat it dry.

4. Heat the olive oil in a large skillet over medium-high heat. When the oil begins to shimmer, add the asparagus and cook, turning the spears every minute or so, until they have firmed up a bit, about 4 minutes. Remove from the heat and set aside.

5. Divide the onion soubise among four plates. Arrange the asparagus on top of the soubise, and then add a poached egg on top of the asparagus. Season the egg with a pinch each of salt and pepper. Garnish with the grated Parmesan, minced chives, and a squeeze of lemon. Eat!

EDAMAME PURÉE

Prep time: **15 minutes**

Cook time: **30 minutes, plus 5 minutes finishing**

Circulator temperature setting: **85°C / 185°F**

1 pound frozen shelled edamame, thawed

1½ cups chicken stock (page 188) or vegetable stock (page 187)

1 teaspoon kosher salt

2 garlic cloves, minced

¼ cup freshly squeezed lemon juice

½ teaspoon freshly grated lemon zest

2 cups packed fresh spinach leaves

Pinch of crushed red pepper flakes

½ cup extra-virgin olive oil

1 sheet nori, toasted and crumbled

I want to show you that healthy sides can be an easy two-step process: a cook time in a bag, and then a puréeing step to create a phenomenally bright accompaniment to many dishes. This purée could be served hot to go with a roasted protein, or chilled to be used in place of hummus or as a condiment on a sandwich. It's versatile, smooth, and delicious.

1. Preheat the circulator water bath to 85°C / 185°F.

2. Place the edamame, chicken stock, salt, garlic, lemon juice, lemon zest, spinach, and red pepper flakes in a resealable gallon-size plastic bag, and seal it using the displacement method (see page 17). Submerge the bag in the circulator water bath and cook for 30 minutes.

3. Remove the bag from the hot water bath and empty the contents into a blender. Run the blender on low speed for 15 to 20 seconds, until the contents have been well puréed. Then, with the blender still running, drizzle in the olive oil. This will emulsify the oil into the purée. Purée until smooth, 10 seconds.

4. Serve the purée immediately, garnished with the crumbled nori. Or, if you prefer, cover and refrigerate it to serve later; the purée will stay fresh in a tightly covered container in the fridge for up to 5 days.

GARLIC-THYME GRILLED ASPARAGUS

Prep time: **10 minutes**

Cook time: **10 minutes, plus 5 minutes finishing**

Circulator temperature setting: **85°C / 185°F**

SERVES 4 AS A SIDE

2 pounds asparagus (the thicker the better—not that pencil-thin stuff)

1 teaspoon freshly grated lemon zest

1 garlic clove, smashed

3 sprigs fresh thyme

2 tablespoons extra-virgin olive oil

Pinch of crushed red pepper flakes

Kosher salt

½ lemon, for serving

Sometimes cooking sous vide is really about consolidating steps or replacing a technique with the immersion time. This recipe would be about the same as blanching asparagus in boiling water and then grilling it, but what the sous vide does is allow the asparagus to cook two-thirds of the way while hanging out with lemon, garlic, and thyme, infusing it with flavor that would be lacking in the boiling water. The grill is a wonderful finish, but I realize that maybe you want to keep it easy . . . go fire up a stovetop grill pan if that is the case.

1. Preheat the circulator water bath to 85°C / 185°F, and preheat your grill or a grill pan to medium-high heat (about 190°C / 375°F).

2. Place the asparagus, lemon zest, garlic, thyme sprigs, olive oil, and red pepper flakes in a resealable gallon-size plastic bag and seal it using the displacement method (see page 17). Submerge the bag in the circulator water bath and cook for 10 minutes.

3. Remove the bag from the hot water bath and remove the asparagus from the bag, discarding the cooking liquid. Pat the asparagus dry with paper towels. Grill the asparagus, turning the spears every minute or so, until they have some nice char marks, about 5 minutes.

4. Transfer the asparagus to a platter and season it with salt to taste. Finish with a good squeeze of lemon juice and serve.

CARAMELIZED CARROTS

(To Be Used a Hundred Ways)

Prep time: **10 minutes**

Cook time: **30 minutes, plus 6 minutes finishing**

Circulator temperature setting: **85°C / 185°F**

SERVES 4 TO 6
AS A SIDE

- 1½ **pounds** young carrots, peeled or scrubbed clean
- 1 **tablespoon** cold unsalted butter, cubed
- 1 **teaspoon** turbinado sugar or honey
- Kosher salt
- 1 **sprig** fresh thyme
- 1 **teaspoon** freshly squeezed lemon juice
- 2 **tablespoons** extra-virgin olive oil

This simple recipe produces a classic sweet-cooked carrot with a touch of caramelization—good on its own and great as a first step. From here, drive forward to a finished dish based on what's in season at the market. Maybe use the carrots in a nice salad with a dollop of yogurt, a handful of pistachios, some pickled onions, and a sprinkling of fresh herbs.

1. Preheat the circulator water bath to 85°C / 185°F.

2. Place the carrots, butter, sugar, a pinch of salt, the thyme sprig, and the lemon juice in a resealable gallon-size plastic bag and seal it using the displacement method (see page 17). Submerge the bag in the circulator water bath and cook for 30 minutes.

3. Five minutes before the carrots are ready, prepare an ice bath.

4. Remove the bag from the hot water bath and immediately transfer it to the ice bath just to shock it and arrest the cooking. (Once it has cooled, the bag of carrots will keep in the fridge for 4 days, and you can start on the next steps when you're ready to serve.)

5. Remove the carrots from the bag and discard any liquids and solids left in the bag. Heat the olive oil in a large skillet over medium heat. When the oil is shimmering, add the carrots in a single layer and cook for 6 minutes, about 2 minutes per side, until they are golden brown and just beginning to char. Do this in batches if you need to prevent crowding.

6. Season with salt to taste and serve or fold into other elements of a dish.

SEARED SWEET POTATOES

with Ginger, Hazelnuts, and Feta

Prep time: **15 minutes**

Cook time: **1 hour, plus 10 minutes finishing**

Circulator temperature setting: **85°C / 185°F**

SERVES 4 AS A SIDE

- **4** medium sweet potatoes, sliced into 1-inch-thick rounds
- **4 tablespoons** (½ stick) unsalted butter
- **1 tablespoon** maple syrup
- **1 teaspoon** kosher salt
- **1 tablespoon** julienned fresh ginger
- **½ cup** raw skinned hazelnuts, crushed
- **2 tablespoons** crumbled feta cheese
- **2 tablespoons** torn fresh mint leaves

UP YOUR SWEET 'TATER GAME.

This is a side, but given the abundance of flavors it can be a complete lunch or a simple dinner all on its own.

1. Preheat the circulator water bath to 85°C / 185°F.

2. Place the sweet potatoes, 2 tablespoons of the butter, and the maple syrup, salt, and ginger in a resealable gallon-size plastic bag and seal it using the displacement method (see page 17). Submerge the bag in the circulator water bath and cook for 1 hour.

3. Remove the bag from the hot water bath and strain the potatoes, discarding the cooking liquids but keeping the ginger.

4. Heat the remaining 2 tablespoons butter in a large cast-iron skillet over high heat. When the butter begins to froth, add the sweet potatoes and ginger and cook until the sweet potatoes begin to brown, about 3 minutes. Flip the potatoes over and cook for 3 minutes more. (If you need to do this in batches, so be it.)

5. To serve, transfer the potatoes to a platter or a large plate. Garnish with the crushed hazelnuts, crumbled feta, and mint leaves. Eat.

HERBY NEW POTATOES

Prep time: **10 minutes**

Cook time: **45 minutes, plus 20 minutes roasting**

Circulator temperature setting: **85°C / 185°F**

SERVES 4 AS A SIDE

- **2 pounds** small new potatoes, left whole
- **1 sprig** fresh rosemary
- **½ tablespoon** chopped fresh sage leaves
- **3 tablespoons** cold unsalted butter, cubed
- **1** garlic clove, halved
- **1 teaspoon** kosher salt, plus more to taste
- **Pinch** of crushed red pepper flakes
- **1 tablespoon** chopped fresh chives
- **½ tablespoon** chopped fresh thyme leaves
- **Pinch** of grated lemon zest

At our farmers' market in Athens, Georgia, you can sometimes find more than ten varieties of potatoes to choose from. When shopping for new potatoes, look for ones that are firm and unblemished. Wash them well before cooking. You can definitely do the sous vide part of this a day or two in advance and then just pull the bag from the fridge and get to the roasting part when you want to eat. Serve the potatoes as a side to a nicely prepared protein or as part of a big veggie spread.

1. Preheat the circulator water bath to 85°C / 185°F.

2. Place the potatoes, rosemary, sage leaves, butter, garlic, and 1 teaspoon salt in a resealable gallon-size plastic bag and seal it using the displacement method (see page 17). Submerge the bag in the circulator water bath and cook for 45 minutes.

3. Preheat your oven to 205°C / 400°F.

4. Remove the bag from the hot water bath and carefully transfer the potatoes to a sheet pan, discarding the cooking liquids, garlic, and herbs. Roast until the potatoes are browned and crispy, about 20 minutes. (Shake the pan a bit every 5 or 10 minutes to keep the potatoes from sticking.)

5. Transfer the potatoes to a medium bowl. Add the red pepper flakes, chives, thyme, and lemon zest. Toss well, season with salt to taste, and serve.

BRAISED SHIITAKE MUSHROOMS

with Fennel and Soy Sauce

Prep time: **10 minutes**

Cook time: **45 minutes, plus 5 minutes finishing**

Circulator temperature setting: **75°C / 167°F**

SERVES 4 AS A SIDE

½ **pound** shiitake mushrooms, stems removed

1 **cup** thinly sliced fennel bulb (sliced against the grain)

2 **tablespoons** chopped fresh fennel fronds

2 **tablespoons** light soy sauce

2 **tablespoons** unsalted butter

1 shallot, thinly sliced

1 **teaspoon** kosher salt

1 **tablespoon** freshly squeezed lemon juice

2 **tablespoons** extra-virgin olive oil

I adore mushrooms, and of the farmed varieties, I am most in love with shiitakes. They are meaty and rich, and so distinctive in flavor. This is a side dish, but to me, with a bowl of rice or some grains, it is pretty much a meal in itself.

1. Preheat the circulator water bath to 75°C / 167°F.

2. If you want, you can break the shiitakes (with your hands) into smaller pieces, about 2 inches each, but don't bruise them too badly. In a medium bowl, combine the mushrooms, sliced fennel, fennel fronds, soy sauce, butter, shallot, salt, lemon juice, and 1 tablespoon of the olive oil. Toss well and transfer everything to a resealable gallon-size plastic bag and seal it using the displacement method (see page 17). Submerge the bag in the circulator water bath and cook for 45 minutes.

3. Heat the remaining 1 tablespoon olive oil in a medium skillet set over high heat. Remove the bag from the hot water bath and transfer the contents to the skillet. Cook until the liquid has reduced to a sauce and the mushrooms are beginning to firm up, about 5 minutes. Serve.

MISO CREAMED CORN

Prep time: **15 minutes**

Cook time: **45 minutes**

Circulator temperature setting: **80°C / 176°F**

SERVES 4 TO 6
AS A SIDE

6 ears fresh corn

½ cup heavy cream

1 tablespoon blond miso

1 teaspoon chopped fresh
tarragon leaves

½ teaspoon kosher salt

1 tablespoon unsalted butter

Creamed corn is a classic, and also the subject of eternal debate. Some factions say that it should not have cream in it, but I kind of like the luxurious feel of the added cream. Corn is so naturally sweet that I wanted to balance that sweetness with some umami in the form of miso, and cooking it sous vide means that none of the cream reduces, keeping the flavor rich but the texture light.

If you want to prepare this in advance, you could shock the bag in ice water after cooking in the hot water bath and then store it in the fridge until you're ready to finish the dish. The corn will stay fresh for 5 days.

1. Preheat the circulator water bath to 80°C / 176°F.

2. On a cutting board, slice the kernels off the ears of corn. Place the corn kernels in a large bowl. Next, one at a time, take a stripped ear of corn, nestle an end in the corn kernels, and run a butter knife up and down to extract all of the corn milk that you can, scraping it into the corn kernels. Add the cream, miso, tarragon, and salt and stir to combine.

3. Place the corn mixture and the butter in a resealable gallon-size plastic bag and seal it using the displacement method (see page 17). Submerge the bag in the circulator water bath and cook for 45 minutes.

4. Remove the bag from the hot water bath and transfer the corn and the cooking liquid to a blender or food processor. Pulse a few times, until the corn is smoother but still a little chunky. It should look like creamed corn. People should see it and exclaim, "Creamed corn!" Serve.

POTATO PURÉE

Prep time: **5 minutes**

Cook time: **1 hour, plus 5 minutes finishing**

Circulator temperature setting: **70°C / 158°F for 15 minutes, then 90°C / 194°F for 45 minutes**

SERVES 4 AS A SIDE

2 pounds peeled Yukon Gold or other waxy potatoes, cut into 1-inch cubes

1 tablespoon kosher salt

½ cup whole milk

¾ pound (3 sticks) top-quality cold unsalted butter, cut into ½-inch cubes

Potato choice here is key. You want a waxy potato that yields smooth, luscious results rather than a starchy potato that results in a floury, fluffy dish. That is the difference between a Yukon Gold and a russet, and I want you to find the former, or a potato in that family, like a Linzer or a German Butterball. The beauty of cooking them sous vide is that they cook slowly in their own juices, not sopping up water in the traditional boiled-potato fashion. And a nice slow cook helps the starches in the potato convert to sugar. It's a process that happens slowly, and the two-temp cook here helps. To make things uniform, I cut the potatoes into 1-inch cubes, but they don't have to be perfect. If you are using young new potatoes or fingerlings, you may want to reduce the cook time a bit, and if you want those little ones peeled, do it while they are still warm after they cook in the bag; the skins will slip off pretty easily at that point.

I weigh the potatoes after peeling when using large Yukons, to ensure that the ratio of potato to butter is correct. Don't let the peeled potatoes spend too much time outside of the water, which can lead to oxidation and browning.

You will need a potato ricer or a food mill to achieve a really smooth purée. Do not use a food processor—you will end up with a gluey mess. If you do not have a ricer, you can let the potatoes cool a touch, grate them with a box grater into a pot, and then place the pot over warm heat and beat in the butter, milk, and the final seasoning of salt.

1. Preheat the circulator water bath to 70°C / 158°F.

2. In a large bowl, combine the potatoes and ½ tablespoon of the salt and toss well. Place the potatoes in a resealable gallon-size plastic bag and seal it using the displacement method (see page 17). Submerge the bag in the circulator water bath and cook for 15 minutes. Then raise the temperature to 90°C / 194°F and once the temperature has been reached, cook for another 45 minutes.

3. Remove the bag from the hot water bath and pour the potatoes onto a clean sheet pan. Let them cool slightly, until they are easier to handle but still hot enough to melt the butter in the next step. While the potatoes are cooling, gently warm the milk in a small saucepan until it is just barely steaming.

4. Using a potato ricer or a food mill, process the potatoes into a medium saucepan. Add the butter and stir to incorporate, emulsifying the butter into the warm potatoes. Add the warm milk and the remaining ½ tablespoon salt (or to taste), and stir until completely combined and smooth. Serve right away.

CARAMELIZED MILK-POACHED PARSNIPS

Prep time: **10 minutes**

Cook time: **45 minutes, plus 5 minutes finishing**

Circulator temperature setting: **85°C / 185°F**

SERVES 4 AS A SIDE

6 parsnips, peeled and halved lengthwise

1 tablespoon unsalted butter

½ cup whole milk

½ teaspoon kosher salt

1 tablespoon extra-virgin olive oil

Parsnips, like turnips, have weathered through some hard times in culinary history, maligned as basic roots, often overcooked, and known as a side of thrifty sustenance rather than a conduit of deliciousness. Their cousin the rutabaga can hold that deserved negative reputation, but parsnips and turnips are fighting back to show that they have been misjudged. This makes me happy because both are delicious.

This recipe is a simple but glorious side to a fall or winter meal.

1. Preheat the circulator water bath to 85°C / 185°F.

2. Place the parsnips, butter, milk, and salt in a resealable gallon-size plastic bag and seal it using the displacement method (see page 17). Submerge the bag in the circulator water bath and cook for 45 minutes.

3. Remove the bag from the hot water bath and transfer the contents to a colander to drain, discarding the liquid. Pat the parsnips dry with paper towels.

4. Heat the olive oil in a large skillet set over medium heat. Arrange the parsnips cut-side down in the skillet and cook, turning them every once in a while, for 5 minutes, or until golden brown. Don't mess with them too much, though, as we are encouraging the caramelization of their sugar content. Transfer them to a platter and serve.

LONG-COOK BROCCOLI

with Chile and Parmesan

Prep time: **10 minutes**

Cook time: **2 hours, plus 5 minutes finishing**

Circulator temperature settomg: **80°C / 176°F**

SERVES 4 AS A SIDE

1 head broccoli (including stalk), cut into florets (see Note)

3 tablespoons extra-virgin olive oil

2 garlic cloves, minced

½ teaspoon crushed red pepper flakes

1 teaspoon kosher salt

1 tablespoon freshly squeezed lemon juice

½ cup chicken stock (page 188)

1 cup finely grated Parmesan cheese

Freshly ground black pepper

———

Note: To prepare the broccoli, trim off just the end of the broccoli stalk. Then cut the broccoli into long-stemmed florets. Cut a slice off one of the stems and chew it. It should be sweet and crisp; if it's tough or stringy, peel the stem with a vegetable peeler until you see that beautiful translucent green, and cut it into bite-size pieces. (There has been a bad habit in cookery of deeming the stalk unworthy of cooking, but it is great.)

Broccoli cooked in an old-school Italian way is a completely different creature than the crisp, barely cooked steamed broccoli that seems to be the way most people cook it. It is broken down, rich and unctuous, buoyed with red pepper flakes and finished with a showering of finely grated Parmesan. It is a keeper of a side dish.

1. Preheat the circulator water bath to 80°C / 176°F.

2. In a large bowl, combine the broccoli, 2 tablespoons of the olive oil, and the garlic, red pepper flakes, salt, lemon juice, and chicken stock. Toss to combine.

3. Place the broccoli mixture in a resealable gallon-size plastic bag and seal it using the displacement method (see page 17). Submerge the bag in the circulator water bath and cook for 2 hours. (This one may be a bit of a floater, due to the irregular shape of the broccoli. Don't worry about it.)

4. When the broccoli is 5 minutes from being done, heat a large cast-iron skillet over medium heat.

5. Remove the bag from the hot water bath and pour the broccoli into a colander set over the sink to drain off the cooking liquid. Set the broccoli aside.

6. Add the remaining 1 tablespoon olive oil to the skillet, and when the oil is shimmering, add the broccoli in a single layer. We are looking to sear and add texture to the broccoli, so just let it go for about 3 minutes, until nicely browned on one side.

7. Transfer the broccoli to a platter and top it with the Parmesan cheese and some freshly ground pepper. Serve.

LONG-COOK CIPOLLINI ONIONS
with Thyme

Prep time: **20 minutes**

Cook time: **2 hours**

Circulator temperature
setting: **85°C / 185°F**

SERVES 6 AS A SIDE

24 cippolini onions, peeled

2 tablespoons unsalted butter

1 sprig fresh thyme

2 teaspoons fresh thyme leaves

2 tablespoons white wine vinegar

Cipollinis look like the flattened golf balls of the allium world. They are a pain to peel, but when you finish cooking them the redemption is sweetness and beauty. This is a silky, harmonious side to a steak, a bottle of good wine, and a group of people whose company you enjoy.

1. Preheat the circulator bath to 85°C / 185°F.

2. Place the onions, butter, thyme sprig, 1 teaspoon of the thyme leaves, and the vinegar in a resealable gallon-size plastic bag and seal it using the displacement method (see page 17). Submerge the bag in the circulator water bath and cook for 2 hours.

3. Remove the bag from the hot water bath. Drain the onions, discarding any liquid and the thyme sprig, and transfer them to a wide serving bowl. Garnish with the remaining 1 teaspoon thyme leaves and serve.

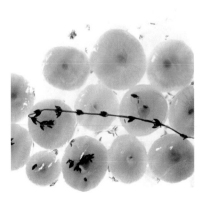

CAULIFLOWER

with Capers, Anchovies,
and Golden Raisins

Prep time: **10 minutes**

Cook time: **20 minutes,
plus 10 minutes finishing**

Circulator temperature
setting: **85°C / 185°F**

SERVES 4 AS A SIDE

4 cups cauliflower florets

¼ cup (½ stick) unsalted butter

2 tablespoons capers

3 canned anchovies, finely chopped

3 tablespoons golden raisins

Kosher salt

1 tablespoon extra-virgin olive oil

1 tablespoon freshly squeezed
    lemon juice

2 tablespoons fresh parsley leaves,
    chopped

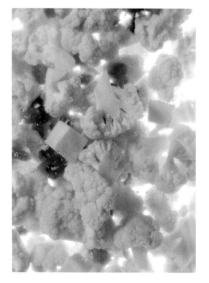

Cauliflower is the new center-of-the-plate vegetable, finally shedding the rancor and divisiveness of being paired with broccoli for the better part of history. This has been a good thing for cauliflower, because being trapped under cheese sauce is not an existence anyone should have to endure.

Capers, anchovies, and raisins hit distinct parts of your palate. Capers have briny salinity; anchovies have complex umami; raisins have concentrated sweetness. When that trio joins with the richness of cauliflower, you have a winner.

1. Preheat the circulator water bath to 85°C / 185°F.

2. Place the cauliflower, butter, capers, anchovies, golden raisins, and a pinch of salt in a resealable gallon-size plastic bag and seal it using the displacement method (see page 17). Submerge the bag in the circulator water bath and cook for 20 minutes.

3. Set a fine-mesh strainer over a large bowl. Remove the bag from the hot water bath and strain the contents through the strainer, reserving the cooking liquid as well as the cauliflower mixture.

4. Heat the olive oil in a large skillet over medium-high heat. When the oil begins to shimmer, add the strained cauliflower mixture. (The anchovies may have dissolved a bit. If you don't see them, that is okay. Their flavor is cooked into the reserved liquid.) Spread it out into a single layer and cook, without stirring, until you see some caramelization on the florets, about 4 minutes. Stir and cook for 4 minutes more, until the cauliflower is nicely browned all over. Remove the skillet from the heat. Add the lemon juice and toss to combine. Season with salt.

5. To serve, transfer the cauliflower mixture to a bowl. Spoon 2 tablespoons of the reserved cooking liquid over the cauliflower and garnish with the parsley.

SWISS CHARD STEMS
on Burrata Toast

Prep time: **10 minutes**

Cook time: **30 minutes**

Circulator temperature
setting: **85°C / 185°F**

SERVES 4 AS A SIDE

2 cups thinly sliced Swiss chard stems

¼ cup cider vinegar

½ cup extra-virgin olive oil

½ teaspoon kosher salt, plus more
to taste

2 tablespoons chopped fresh parsley
leaves and stems

1 tablespoon freshly grated
orange zest

4 slices of your favorite bread

4 balls burrata cheese

Chefs have been adjusting to a new world of food, and we are learning to cook cuts and parts that we used to throw away in great abundance. The tops of leeks get dried and powdered, the flowers of basil are garnish, the pits of peaches are made into vinegars. We are doing all of this to sustain our food systems, to waste less, and to derive the most economic output from our pantries. We are a curious bunch, so that helps, and what we're finding is that many of these things are very, very delicious.

This recipe takes chard stems, often thrown away, and slowly cooks them in a wash of olive oil and vinegar until they are silky. They are so good piled high over rich burrata mozzarella, a cheese that was once a rarified treat but now is available even at my regular grocery in Athens, Georgia. Regular fresh mozzarella will work in a pinch as well, though it won't collapse so seductively.

1. Preheat the circulator water bath to 85°C / 185°F.

2. Place the Swiss chard stems, vinegar, olive oil, ½ teaspoon salt, parsley, and orange zest in a resealable gallon-size plastic bag and seal it using the displacement method (see page 17). Submerge the bag in the circulator water bath and cook for 30 minutes.

3. Five minutes before the Swiss chard has finished cooking, toast your favorite sliced bread according to your liking. Once it has cooled slightly, transfer the toast to four plates.

4. Remove the bag from the hot water bath and let it cool for 2 to 3 minutes. Then pour the Swiss chard into a bowl.

5. To serve, place a ball of burrata on top of each slice of toast and break the skin to let the cheese collapse in its opulent fashion. Season the burrata with a pinch of salt. Spoon the Swiss chard on top of the burrata and season with salt to taste. Dive in.

SUNCHOKE SOUP

with Almonds and Olives

Prep time: **20 minutes**

Cook time: **4 hours, plus 5 minutes finishing**

Circulator temperature setting: **80°C / 176°F**

MAKES 2 QUARTS

- **1 tablespoon** unsalted butter
- **2 shallots**, minced
- **1 tablespoon** freshly squeezed lemon juice
- **1 pound** sunchokes, scrubbed
- **2 cups** whole milk
- **3 cups** chicken stock (page 188)
- **1 teaspoon** fresh thyme leaves, chopped
- **2 bay leaves**
- **1 teaspoon** kosher salt, plus more to taste
- **¼ cup** sliced unsalted almonds, toasted
- **¼ cup** chopped pitted green olives
- **2 tablespoons** extra-virgin olive oil

Cooking in a half-gallon mason jar is easy, and though the wait time on this is a bit longer than you would think for a soup, it is super-simple prep work and then you go do whatever you want. I recommend a crossword or a walk.

Sunchokes, also known as Jerusalem artichokes and farty tubers, can be peeled or not peeled, but if you follow the latter direction, just make sure they are scrubbed clean under cold water.

Also, if you have never seen sunchoke plants on a farm, with their wispy thin stalks reaching gracefully skyward with tender yellow flowers, you really are missing out on botanical beauty.

1. Preheat the circulator water bath to 80°C / 176°F, with the water line just a couple of inches shy of the height of a 2-quart mason jar.

2. Heat a small skillet over medium heat and add the butter. When the butter bubbles and froths, add the shallots and cook, stirring occasionally, until the shallots are nicely colored and cooked down, about 2 minutes. Remove from the heat and set aside.

3. Fill a bowl halfway with cold water and add the lemon juice. On a cutting board, thinly slice the sunchokes (about ¼ inch thick), and as you finish cutting each one, drop the slices into the lemon water. (This will prevent oxidation, which happens quickly with sunchokes.) Once all of the sunchokes are in the acidulated water, drain them and transfer them to a 2-quart mason jar. Add the reserved shallots and the milk, chicken stock, thyme, bay leaves, and 1 teaspoon salt. Cap the jar with the lid and band, tightening it finger-tight, and place the jar in the circulator water bath. The water should reach the fill level of the jar; add more water to the bath if necessary. Cook for 4 hours,

adding water if needed to maintain the level. (Or cover the bath with plastic wrap.)

4. Remove the jar from the hot water bath and pour the contents into a blender. Purée until smooth, and add more salt to taste.

5. Set a conical fine-mesh sieve over a saucepan and strain the soup into the pan. Keep the soup warm until ready to serve. When serving, garnish each portion with some of the almonds, green olives, and a drizzle of olive oil.

ABSINTHE-BRAISED FENNEL

with Grapefruit, Green Olives,
and Pickled Fennel Stems

Prep time: **10 minutes**

Cook time: **30 minutes, plus 15 minutes finishing**

Circulator temperature setting: **85°C / 185°F**

SERVES 4 AS A SIDE

2 tablespoons absinthe or Pernod

1 large fennel bulb, stems trimmed and reserved for pickling (recipe follows), bulb cored and cut into ¼-inch-wide slices

2 tablespoons unsalted butter

1 teaspoon kosher salt

2 grapefruits, peeled (all pith removed) and cut into ¼-inch-thick rounds

3 tablespoons coarsely chopped pitted meaty green olives, such as Cerignola or Castelvetrano

3 tablespoons Pickled Fennel Stems (recipe follows)

1 teaspoon chopped fresh fennel fronds

Absinthe, "the green fairy" of liqueurs, has a wonderful flavor that has a beautiful kinship with fennel and lays the foundation for this vibrant salad. The grapefruit is a great acidic foil, and the olives play saline brine, and the pickled stems add texture and a final pucker.

1. Preheat the circulator water bath to 85°C / 185°F.

2. In a small saucepan, heat the absinthe over medium heat until it is simmering. Remove the pan from the heat. Using a long-handled lighter, carefully light the absinthe to burn off some of the alcohol. After 45 seconds, place a lid on the pan to extinguish the flame. (There should be some liquid left, but with most of the alcohol cooked off.) Let the liquid cool to room temperature.

3. Place the absinthe, fennel slices, butter, and salt in a resealable gallon-size plastic bag and seal it using the displacement method (see page 17). Submerge the bag in the circulator water bath and cook for 30 minutes.

4. Remove the bag from the hot water bath. Remove the fennel from the bag and set it aside in a small bowl, reserving the liquid in the plastic bag. Place the resealed bag in the refrigerator and let it chill for 10 minutes to allow the butter to solidify a bit.

≫→ *Recipe continues*

5. Once the butter has begun to congeal, strain the braising liquid through a fine-mesh strainer into a clean container. Discard the solids and set the strained braising liquid aside.

6. To serve, arrange the grapefruit slices on individual plates, and then add the braised fennel over the grapefruit. Sprinkle the chopped olives, pickled fennel stems, and fennel fronds on top. Lastly, spoon some of the reserved braising liquid over the plate to dress everything evenly.

PICKLED FENNEL STEMS

Makes 1 pint

You'll need to make these pickled stems at least a day before you plan to use them, but do it: They are a sure-fire winner.

2 cups cider vinegar

¼ cup sugar

1 teaspoon kosher salt

1 tablespoon whole black peppercorns

⅛ teaspoon crushed red pepper flakes

1 tablespoon yellow mustard seeds

Stem from 1 fennel bulb, with small stems and fronds removed, sliced into ⅛-inch-thick rounds (about 2 cups)

In a small saucepan, combine 1 cup of water with the vinegar, sugar, salt, peppercorns, red pepper flakes, and mustard seeds. Bring to a boil over medium heat, whisking to dissolve the sugar and salt. Remove the pan from the heat and let the pickling liquid cool to room temperature.

Place the sliced fennel stems in a clean 1-pint mason jar. Pour the pickling liquid and seasonings over the sliced fennel stems and cap the jar with the lid and band, tightening the band just to finger-tight.

Refrigerate the fennel stems for 24 hours before serving. They will keep for about 1 week.

ONION SOUBISE

Prep time: **10 minutes**

Cook time: **12 hours, plus 5 minutes finishing**

Circulator temperature setting: **85°C / 185°F**

SERVES 4 TO 8;
MAKES ABOUT
3 CUPS

3 sweet yellow onions, thinly sliced

¼ cup long-grain white rice

3 tablespoons unsalted butter

1 cup heavy cream

2 teaspoons kosher salt

This name is actually redundant, because *soubise* is an onion sauce, but for clarity's sake this is how we usually list it on menus. Seems a little odd to have such a basic purée—made with onions, cream, and rice—named after an eighteenth-century aristocrat, the Prince of Soubise, but who knows? Maybe he was a wonderful and yet simple person. Soubise is a testament to the simple beauty of the onion; it pairs well with pretty much everything and should be a staple in your arsenal of culinary knowledge. This one takes a while, but onions love the long haul, and the sweetness you get out of them is amazing.

It's a terrific sauce for simply cooked chicken, fish, or meats. What doesn't a creamy onion purée go with?

1. Preheat the circulator water bath to 85°C / 185°F.

2. Place the onions, rice, butter, cream, and salt in a resealable gallon-size plastic bag and seal it using the displacement method (see page 17). Submerge the bag in the circulator water bath and cook for 12 hours, adding water as necessary to maintain the level.

3. Carefully remove the bag from the hot water bath and transfer the contents to a blender. Blend on high speed for 1 minute or until completely smooth. Transfer the purée to a serving dish and serve it immediately, or let the soubise cool before storing it in an airtight container in the fridge. It will keep for 3 days.

BUTTER-BRAISED RADISHES

with Za'atar

Prep time: **15 minutes**

Cook time: **25 minutes**

Circulator temperature
setting: **85°C / 185°F**

SERVES 4 AS A SIDE

2 bunches medium-size red radishes,
greens removed, quartered

¼ **cup** (½ stick) unsalted butter

Freshly grated zest of 1 lemon

2 teaspoons za'atar (recipe follows,
or use store-bought)

Pinch of Maldon sea salt

This is a simple buttery braise of radishes. *Who braises radishes?* I do. And you should. They are so good when cooked—they lose their heat but keep their creaminess. Za'atar, a simple blend of four ingredients, is ubiquitous in Middle Eastern cooking and should find a place in your regular culinary regimen. You can buy it if need be, but it is easy to make. The blend of lemony sumac, thyme, salt, and sesame is a study in balance and works perfectly in this recipe to give substance and nuttiness to the radishes.

1. Preheat the circulator water bath to 85°C / 185°F.

2. Place the radishes, butter, and lemon zest in a resealable gallon-size plastic bag and seal it using the displacement method (see page 17). Submerge the bag in the circulator water bath and cook for 25 minutes.

3. Remove the bag from the hot water bath and strain the radishes in a colander set over a bowl, reserving the cooking liquid. Transfer the radishes to a medium bowl.

4. Add the za'atar and sea salt to the radishes and toss well to combine.

5. To serve, place the radishes in a serving bowl and spoon 2 tablespoons of the reserved cooking liquid on top. Eat!

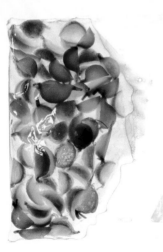

ZA'ATAR

Makes about 1 cup

2 tablespoons chopped fresh thyme leaves

2 tablespoons white sesame seeds, toasted

1 tablespoon ground sumac

½ teaspoon kosher salt

Combine the thyme, sesame seeds, sumac, and salt in a small jar with a tight-fitting lid and shake to combine. The za'atar will stay fresh in the fridge for about a week.

SPICED RED WINE-POACHED PEARS

Prep time: **15 minutes**

Cook time: **1 hour, plus 15 minutes finishing**

Circulator temperature setting: **83°C / 181.4°F**

SERVES 4

4 pears, stemmed and cored but left whole (Bosc pears work great here)

2 **cups** dry red wine

¼ **cup** sorghum molasses

½ **cup** sugar

5 bay leaves

3 star anise pods

I have been making poached pears for decades, and I never tire of them. You can serve them with ice cream, a simple pound cake, or just with some whipped cream or sour cream or yogurt. This dessert is a stunning one to impress people as well, and if you want to extend its use, reduce some of the poaching liquid down to use in a simple cocktail. I will take a poached pear mimosa over a traditional mimosa every darn day of the week.

1. Preheat the circulator water bath to 83°C / 181.4°F.

2. Place the pears, red wine, molasses, sugar, bay leaves, and star anise pods in a resealable gallon-sized plastic bag and seal it using the displacement method (see page 17). Submerge the bag in the circulator water bath and cook for 1 hour.

3. Remove the bag from the hot water bath, carefully remove the pears, and transfer them to a large plate. Pour the poaching liquid (including the bay leaves and star anise pods) into a large saucepan set over medium-high heat. Simmer for 15 minutes to reduce the poaching liquid to 1 cup. Once it has reduced, drizzle the reduction on top of the pears and serve.

CELERY THREE WAYS

with Almonds and Parmesan

Prep time: **15 minutes**

Cook time: **45 minutes**

Circulator temperature setting: **85°C / 185°F**

SERVES 4 AS A SIDE

10 celery stalks

1 cup chicken stock (page 188) or vegetable stock (page 187)

½ teaspoon kosher salt

1 tablespoon freshly grated lemon zest

4 tablespoons fresh celery leaves (pale green leaves only)

2 tablespoons freshly squeezed lemon juice

Fine sea salt

1 teaspoon extra-virgin olive oil

¼ cup shaved Parmesan cheese

¼ cup Marcona almonds, chopped

It is odd how celery flies under the fancy-food radar and is deemed so conventional, just a simple member of the *mirepoix* gang. To me, celery has a distinctive flavor and complexity, and it loves being cooked. Think of the first time you had cooked celery: It was probably in Thanksgiving stuffing or in a steamy paper container of takeout Chinese stir-fry. Think about how the celery stands out. Give the celery respect, because no respectable stuffing, chicken salad, Bloody Mary, or chicken wing setup would be complete without the celery.

This is a simple side but one that also qualifies for a fancy dinner. It is a keeper.

1. Preheat the circulator water bath to 85°C / 185°F.

2. Take 8 celery stalks, peel them with a vegetable peeler to remove the fibers, and cut them into ½-inch-thick slices. Place the sliced celery in a resealable gallon-size plastic bag, add the chicken stock, kosher salt, and lemon zest, and seal the bag using the displacement method (see page 17). Submerge the bag in the circulator water bath and cook for 45 minutes.

3. Meanwhile, peel the remaining 2 celery stalks and cut them into ⅛-inch-wide slices.

4. Remove the bag from the hot water bath and drain the celery, discarding the liquid.

5. In a medium bowl, combine the braised celery, the uncooked celery, and the celery leaves. Add the lemon juice and season with sea salt to taste. Add the olive oil, Parmesan, and almonds, and toss again to coat. Serve.

APPLESAUCE

Prep time: **30 minutes**

Cook time: **2 hours, plus 5 minutes finishing**

Circulator temperature setting: **80°C / 176°F**

MAKES 1 QUART

- **8 medium** apples (a crisp variety such as Arkansas Blacks, Pink Lady, or Granny Smith)
- **2 tablespoons** sugar
- **1 teaspoon** freshly grated lemon zest
- **2 tablespoons** freshly squeezed lemon juice
- **1 teaspoon** ground cinnamon
- **½ teaspoon** freshly ground cumin seeds
- **½ teaspoon** ground nutmeg
- **½ teaspoon** ground allspice
- **2 tablespoons** unsalted butter, at room temperature

I have always loved applesauce. It was what we ate with pork chops. Being raised by a single father who really should never have been cooking food (he was an economist) made me treasure a couple of the basics that made food palatable, and applesauce was one of them. But this homemade version is so easy and so good. Sous vide is the cure to over-reduced or burned applesauce—and it just keeps all the flavors from evaporating away. The spices make it a bit more savory—great on a ham sandwich or a throwback homage on pork chops. It's also great on plain yogurt with maple syrup and granola in the morning.

My favorite apples of all time are Arkansas Blacks, but you can use whatever looks good at the store. Look for crisp, firm, and American. Like The Rock.

1. Preheat the circulator water bath to 80°C / 176°F.

2. Peel and core the apples, then cut them into a large dice.

3. In a medium bowl, combine the apples, sugar, lemon zest, and lemon juice and toss to combine. Add the cinnamon, cumin seeds, nutmeg, allspice, and butter and stir until the apples are evenly coated.

4. Place the apple mixture in a resealable gallon-size plastic bag and seal it using the displacement method (see page 17). Submerge the bag in the circulator water bath and cook for 2 hours.

5. Remove the bag from the hot water bath and let it cool slightly. Then pour the contents of the bag into a blender and blend until smooth. Serve, or store in a tightly covered mason jar in the fridge. It will keep in the fridge for about 2 weeks.

EARL GREY-LEMON POACHED PLUMS

Prep time: **20 minutes**

Cook time: **30 minutes, plus 5 minutes finishing**

Circulator temperature setting: **83°C / 181.4°F**

SERVES 6

1 cup sugar

4 (1-inch-wide) strips lemon zest

1 guajillo chile

1 teaspoon mustard seeds

3 Earl Grey tea bags

6 plums, halved and pitted

I love poached stone fruit, and plums are my jam. I would buy medium-size plums for this—about the size of a squash ball, which is smaller than a baseball but bigger than a golf ball. This dessert is wonderful served warm with vanilla ice cream or chilled and served with luscious Greek yogurt.

1. Preheat the circulator water bath to 83°C / 181.4°F.

2. Combine the sugar, lemon zest, guajillo chile, mustard seeds, and 2 cups of water in a medium saucepan. Bring to a boil over high heat and add the Earl Grey tea bags. Remove the pan from the heat and let the tea steep for 5 minutes. Then remove the tea bags and let the poaching liquid cool.

3. Place the poaching liquid and the plums in a resealable gallon-size plastic bag and seal it using the displacement method (see page 17). Submerge the bag in the circulator water bath and cook for 30 minutes.

4. Remove the bag from the hot water bath and pour the poaching liquid and the plums into a large skillet. Cook over medium-high heat until the poaching liquid is reduced to a sauce, about 5 minutes.

5. Transfer the plums and sauce to a rimmed plate and serve hot or cold.

MANGO BUTTER

Prep time: **10 minutes**

Cook time: **3 hours**

Circulator temperature
setting: **85°C / 185°F**

MAKES 1 QUART

3 large ripe mangoes, peeled, pitted, and diced

½ **cup** sugar

1 teaspoon freshly grated lemon zest

1 teaspoon freshly grated orange zest

Pinch of cayenne pepper

1 teaspoon instant powdered pectin

I love fruit butters. They are luscious versions of jam, smooth in consistency and rich in fruit flavor. Making them sous vide keeps them fresh tasting by holding all the cooking liquids and aromas safely vaulted up in the bag. There are many types of mangoes, but I would use the pretty large ones we see in most grocery stores. Make sure they are ripe.

This mango butter loves toast.

1. Preheat the circulator water bath to 85°C / 185°F.

2. Combine the mangoes, sugar, lemon zest, orange zest, and cayenne in a large bowl and toss well to combine.

3. Place the mango mixture in a large resealable gallon-size plastic bag and seal it using the displacement method (see page 17). Submerge the bag in the circulator water bath and cook for 3 hours.

4. Remove the bag from the hot water bath and pour the mixture into a saucepan. Bring it to a quick boil, add the pectin, and stir to incorporate. Then remove the pan from the heat and let the mixture cool.

5. Transfer the mango butter to a clean jar and store it in the fridge for up to 10 days.

ACKNOWLEDGMENTS

Writing books is a team effort, because a cookbook is one part writing and nine parts other things. My team on this book was a wonder of efficiency and professionalism: Andrew Thomas Lee, friend and photographer; Samantha Sanford, prop and food stylin'; Matthew Palmerlee, cooking partner; and Taylor Rogers, possessor of sunny disposition and vast organizational skills. Valerie Lynch carried the book over the finish line and got it into the capable hands of my editor, Francis Lam, and the awesome publishing team at Clarkson Potter/Random House. That group includes Doris Cooper, Marysarah Quinn, Christine Tanigawa, Mark McCauslin, Heather Williamson, Lydia O'Brien, and designer Ian Dingman. I told you it was a team effort.

Rani Bolton at Inland Seafood always delivers the goods. Nomiku, All-Clad, and Anova kept the water warm. Dave Yasuda at Snake River Farms is a super human of American Kobe beef. Many wonderful farms, too many to list, have their produce and hard work featured in the dishes.

Kate Kiefer and Alice Lee provided their home kitchen for our photo shoots and ate leftovers with care and gusto.

Many fine people tested the recipes and provided invaluable feedback: Anthony Rue, Cameron Gatter, Cornelius Bouknight, Grace Chiu, Jessica Vizzutti, Joe Pierzchajlo, Maddie Swab, Michael Hughes, Reba Toloday, Ryan Duckworth, and Todd Case.

To all of my employees at the restaurants: Thank you for being beacons of hospitality.

And as always, a huge hug to the people I adore more than anything in this world, Beatrice and Clementine.

Published in the United States by Clarkson Potter/Publishers,
an imprint of Random House, a division of Penguin
Random House LLC, New York.
clarksonpotter.com

CLARKSON POTTER is a trademark and POTTER
with colophon is a registered trademark of Penguin Random
House LLC.

Library of Congress Cataloging-in-Publication Data
Names: Acheson, Hugh, author.
Title: Sous vide: better home cooking / Hugh Acheson.
Description: First edition. | New York: Clarkson Potter, 2019
Identifiers: LCCN 2019000701 (print) | LCCN 2019000802 (ebook) |
    ISBN 9781984822291 (Ebook) | ISBN 9781984822284
Subjects: LCSH: Sous-vide cooking. | LCGFT: Cookbooks.
Classification: LCC TX690.7 (ebook) | LCC TX690.7 .A27 2019
    (print) | DDC 641.5/87—dc23
LC record available at https://lccn.loc.gov/2019000701.

ISBN 978-1-984-82228-4
Ebook ISBN 978-1-984-82229-1

Printed in China

Book and cover design by Ian Dingman
Photographs by Andrew Thomas Lee

10 9 8 7 6 5 4 3 2 1

First Edition

2|20-1
7/20-1